Discovering
Sierra Trees

by
Stephen F. Arno

illustrated by
Jane Gyer

Published by
Yosemite Association
and
Sequoia Natural History Association
In Cooperation with the National Park Service
1973

ACKNOWLEDGEMENTS

The author would like to thank numerous people who have supplied encouragement, information, and reviews that helped shape this publication. Bill Jones, Jack and Jane Gyer, and Henry Berrey, affiliated with Yosemite National Park, and John Palmer of Sequoia were instrumental in managing this production. Several other individuals on the staffs of Yosemite and Sequoia-Kings Canyon National Parks; the Yosemite and Sequoia Natural History Associations; and the Sequoia, Sierra, Inyo, Toiyabe, and Stanislaus National Forests were also quite helpful. Thanks is also extended to Mary DeDecker of Independence, to Dr. Harold Biswell and Winni Kessler of the University of California at Berkeley, and to Harold Basey.

INTRODUCTION

Nearly half a century after throngs of boisterous gold-seekers had combed the Sierra Nevada, naturalist John Muir puzzled:

"The coniferous forest of the Sierra are the grandest and most beautiful in the world, and grow in a delightful climate on the most interesting and accessible of mountain-ranges, yet strange to say they are not well known."

A staid scientist today would have to concur that the Sierra forests rank among the most magnificent on earth, and that as Muir observed they contrast with most of the world's other great forests in their inviting, sunlit openness.

Considering that a sizeable number of California's 20,000,000 inhabitants now flock to the Sierra woodlands and forests the year-around, Muir's statement about their not being well known might no longer seem true. However, there is a vast difference between merely visiting these forests and truly "knowing them"; and though millions ride and tramp through these woods, they still "are not well known."

It is our hope that this book will illuminate one facet of the Sierra forests by bringing out the character or "natural history" of each of the approximately three dozen species of native trees found here. Our book describes forests and trees inhabiting the western and eastern slopes of the central and southern Sierra Nevada from Tuolumne and Mono Counties southward. Much of this beautiful forest region is owned in trust for the American public and is managed by the U. S. Forest Service (Stanislaus, Sierra, Sequoia, Toiyabe, and Inyo National Forests) and the National Park Service (Yosemite, Kings Canyon, and Sequoia National Parks).

The Sierra forests make a fascinating study for many reasons, perhaps most outstanding being their diversity of trees. Valley oak, cottonwoods, sycamore, and a host of other broadleaved trees grow along the lowermost flanks of the Sierra's west slope, just a few hundred feet above sea level. One must climb two vertical miles through several climatic zones occupied by a variety of broadleaf woodlands, the "elfin forest" or chaparral, as well as coniferous forests before he at last emerges from the tree-dominated landscape at timberline. Continuing his rugged journey eastward over the glistening granite crest of the Sierra, he will then enter and descend one mile vertically through a strikingly different type of forest perched on the range's spectacular east escarpment, high above purplish deserts of the Great Basin.

The Sierra Nevada's rich forest community can be described as a sort of "melting pot" where trees from half a dozen diverse climatic regions meet. The mild "Mediterranean" environment of California provides Digger pine, California torreya, the oaks, sycamore, California-laurel, and California buckeye. These species are largely restricted to the western skirts of the Sierra. The California mountain climatic region contributes some magnificent conifers: giant sequoia, jeffrey and sugar pines, red fir, and incense-cedar. Several trees that thrive along the cool and rainy North Pacific Coast extend southward into the Sierra, where they are confined to higher elevations or moist sites. Western white pine, Douglas-fir, mountain hemlock, bigleaf maple, and Pacific dogwood are the North Coast species. Lodgepole pine and quaking aspen are representatives of the Canadian boreal forest. Still other trees spread westward to the Sierra from the Rocky Mountains; these include ponderosa and whitebark pines, white fir, and water birch.

Finally, another sizeable group, characteristic of the arid mountains of the Great Basin and the Southwest, prospers on the Sierra's eastern or desert slope. Here are the pinyon, junipers, foxtail and limber pines, Fremont cottonwood, desert ash, and mountain mahogany. The centerpiece (pages 41 & 42) shows a greatly simplified view of the composition of our Sierra forests.

Another interesting aspect of Sierra Nevada forests is the immensity of the trees that grow here. In addition to giant sequoia, world's largest tree (maximum: 26'9" thick at 4½' above ground level, and 272' tall), the southern Sierra harbors the world's largest known pine — a sugar pine 10' thick and 216' tall. Other trees that attain their largest-known proportions growing in the southern Sierra include Jeffrey pine (7½' x 175'), foxtail pine (8½' x 70'), lodgepole pine (6'9" x 91'), mountain hemlock (7½' x 113'), western juniper (13½' x 87'), white fir (8'10" x 179'), and California red fir (8½' x 180').

We hope this guidebook to exploration of Sierra trees will stimulate some readers to delve deeper into the subject of Sierra forests. For instance, what about their ecology? Can they be conserved or must they be sacrificed in parts to meet our insatiable demands for more land to live upon, more outdoor recreation facilities, more wood products, more water, and other public "needs"? The combined efforts of countless well-informed conservationists over the past century have been responsible for creation and protection of the Sierra forest reserves and parks that we enjoy today. But the challenge to maintain the quality of the outdoors has never been greater.

Many fine publications provide detailed information on the Sierra and its trees; the following list makes a good beginning:

Griffin, James R. and Wm. Critchfield. *The Distribution of Forest Trees in California*. U.S. Dept. Agr., Forest Service, Research Paper PSW-82/1972. 114 pp.

Munz, Philip A. *A California Flora*. Univ. of Calif. Press. 1959, and a supplement issued in 1968. 1681 pp.

Muir, John. *The Mountains of California*. Doubleday Anchor, paperback. 1961. (originally publ. in 1894) 300 pp.

Sudworth, George B. *Forest Trees of the Pacific Slope*. U. S. Dept. Agriculture, Forest Service. 1908. (a classic, recently reprinted in paperback by Dover Publ. Co.) 441 pp.

Peattie, Donald C. *A Natural History of Western Trees*. Houghton Mifflin Co. 1953. 751 pp.

U.S. Forest Service. *Silvics of Forest Trees of the United States*. Agriculture Handbook 271, U.S. Gov't Printing Off. 1965. 762 pp.

Leopold, Aldo. *A Sand County Almanac* (and sketches here and there). Oxford Univ. Press. 1949. (the delightful classic of modern conservation literature, available in inexpensive paperback) 226 pp.

Table of Contents

CONIFERS:

1. Digger pine (*Pinus sabiniana*) 1
2. knobcone pine (*P. attenuata*) 3
3. singleleaf pinyon (*P. monophylla*) 5
4. ponderosa pine (*P. ponderosa*) 7
5. Jeffrey pine (*P. jeffreyi*) 10
6. sugar pine (*P. lambertiana*) 12
7. western white pine (*P. monticola*) 15
8. lodgepole pine (*P. contorta* var. *murrayana*) 17
9. whitebark pine (*P. albicaulis*) 20
10. limber pine (*P. flexilis*) 22
11. foxtail pine (*P. balfouriana*) 24
12. white fir (*Abies concolor*) 27
13. red fir (*A. magnifica* & var. *shastensis*) 29
14. Douglas-fir (*Pseudotsuga menziesii*) 32
15. mountain hemlock (*Tsuga mertensiana*) 35
16. giant sequoia (*Sequoiadendron giganteum*) 37
17. incense-cedar (*Calocedrus decurrens*) 44
18. western juniper (*Juniperus occidentalis*) 47
19. California torreya (*Torreya californica*) 50

BROADLEAVES:

1. tree willows (*Salix* — 5 species) 52
2. black cottonwood (*Populus trichocarpa*) 55
3. quaking aspen (*Populus tremuloides*) 58
4. white alder (*Alnus rhombifolia*) 61
5. water birch (*Betula occidentalis*) 63
6. Calif. white oak (*Quercus lobata*) 65
7. blue oak (*Q. douglasii*) 68
8. Calif. black oak (*Q. kelloggii*) 70
9. live oaks (*Q. chrysolepis* & *Q. wislizenii*) 72
10. Calif. sycamore (*Platanus racemosa*) 74
11. California-laurel (*Umbellularia californica*) 76
12. bigleaf maple (*Acer macrophyllum*) 78
13. Calif. buckeye (*Aesculus californica*) 80
14. ash (*Fraxinus* — 3 species) 82
15. Pacific dogwood (*Cornus nuttallii*) 83
16. wild cherry (*Prunus* — 3 species) 85
17. mountain-mahogany (*Cercocarpus* — 2 species) . 85

Digger pine

Pinus sabiniana
Pine family (*Pinaceae*)

Solitary, spreading and open-crowned grayish pine growing on the torrid lower slopes of California's green and golden foothills.

Digger pine characterizes the sub-tropical foothill environment on the lower slopes of the Sierra Nevada in the historic land of the Mother Lode. Nearly a century ago John Muir, the colorful western natural-ist, observed that few people seeing a Digger pine for the first time would take it to be a conifer of any kind because of its sparse foliage and open crown that branches more like an elm. "No other tree of my acquaintance," he wrote, "so sub-stantial in body is in foliage so thin and so pervious to the light. The sunbeams sift through even the leafiest trees with scarcely any interruption . . ."

Pioneer California botanist Willis Jepson added that Digger pine is, "Scarcely in any sense a beautiful tree, offering no comfort of shade to the inexperienced wayfarer who, dusty and sun-bitten, seeks its protection; scorned, too, by the lumbermen, it is nevertheless, the most interesting and picturesque tree of the foothills . . ."

Digger pine, which is the most common conifer in the California foothills, inhabits the western slope of the Sierra from about 1000 to 4000 feet elevation. It is absent from the foothills west of Sequoia and Kings Canyon National Parks, although it grows both north and south of that area. Digger pine does not occupy the Sierra's eastern or "desert" slope.

Although it attains only modest size in comparison with most other Cali-fornia pines, the distinctive spread-ing crowns of Digger pines overtop blue oaks and most of the other trees with which they grow. Unlike other pines which grow vertically, Digger pine has a way of leaning out at right angles to the hillsides. These trees often reach 60 feet in height and two feet in diameter in the scant 60-80 years which is their normal lifespan.

Far more remarkable is the large size of their needles and cones. The needle-like leaves are borne in clusters of three and grow 8-12 inches long, while the almost spherical cones weigh up to four pounds when green. The tip of each cone scale is drawn out into a stout, sharp claw, probably a natural adaptation to protect the plump, nut-like seeds nestled in pockets at the base of each cone scale. This armor is sufficiently vicious to make it hazardous for humans wearing light shoes to walk carelessly about beneath the pines, and even auto-mobile tires have reputedly been damaged when driven over the cones. Nevertheless, western gray squirrels are adept at gnawing off the claw-like scales and pilfering the nuts, which at 750/lb. are al-most twice the size of pinyon pine nuts.

Some of the first pioneers to reach California dubbed Indians they met in the Central Valley "Diggers" because roots and bulbs (corms) comprised much of their diet. When these newcomers learned that the native Californians subsisted upon the large, rich seeds of a foothill pine during part of the year, they called the tree "Digger pine"; it is also known appropriately as "gray pine", and as "bull pine".

John Muir described the Digger pine nut harvest as follows:
"The (Indian) men climb the trees like bears and beat off the cones with sticks . . . while the squaws gather the big, generous cones, and roast them until the scales open sufficiently to allow the hard-shelled seeds to be beaten out. Then in the cool evenings, men, women, and children, with their capacity for dirt greatly increased by the soft resin with which they are all bedraggled, form circles around camp-fires, on the bank of the nearest stream, and lie in easy independence cracking nuts and laughing and chattering, as heedless of the future as the squirrels."

Understandably the California Indians treasured this gray-green pine. White settlers, however, considered it worthless and often hacked it down since unlike other pines its wood was usable only as fuel. Thankfully, more Americans today seem willing to leave room in their world for the curious spreading pines that grow scattered among the fields of grass and flowers and with the oaks along highways winding through the Sierra foothills.

Digger pine
Pinus sabiniana

knobcone pine

Pinus attenuata
Pine family (*Pinaceae*)

An obscure little pine scattered about in hot, rocky sites at lower elevations in the mountains of northern California and southwestern Oregon.

Knobcone pine is a hard-to-find tree that only a small proportion of botanists and foresters have ever seen growing in its natural habitat. It occupies many areas of northern California, but is seldom abundant. With only this information in mind one might logically conclude that knobcone grows hidden away among lofty ridges and crags at timberline. Actually, knobcone grows at lower elevations (1500-5500') on sun-scorched rocky ridges often too hot and dry for the trees that characterize the conifer forest zone.

In the Sierra Nevada, knobcone forms small groves of strange little trees, their gray-green crowns poking out from a sea of chaparral (tall foothill shrubs) and scrubby oaks.

The crown looks as though it is covered with burs; these are the cones, which never fall off. *Knobcone is rare in the Sierra, growing only in a few locations along the west slope of the mountains southward to Yosemite. There it can be seen along the fire road to Deer Camp, the old Coulterville Road above Big Meadow, and the Merced River at El Portal.*

Western trees have evolved in the presence of lightning-caused forest fires through millions of years. Most of our species of pines as well as many other magnificent trees are largely dependent upon such recurring natural conflagrations for their very existence. Without fire, duff and dense undergrowth accumulates on the forest floor making a poor seed bed for most conifers. The canopy of tall trees gradually blocks out nearly all direct sunlight. Only a few conifers such as incense-cedar and white fir can reproduce under dense shade and heavy duff; thus without periodic burns the rich mixture of towering pines and sequoia would eventually disappear.

It is easy to see how natural fire benefits the huge ponderosa and sugar pines, Douglas-firs, and sequoias — sheathed in an armor of thick, flame-resistant bark — as it burns away the duff and undergrowth and opens up the stand for young trees. Knobcone pine also needs fire to survive in nature, but knobcone *is not* a fire-resistant tree and is almost invariably killed by the flames. This seemingly strange situation is actually rather common among trees and shrubs; many species that are highly vulnerable to fire need it in order to reproduce. Some of these fire-dependent species sprout after being burned or need flames to get rid of the organic litter and to expose mineral soil for their seeds. Fire may be necessary to destroy competing vegetation or to scarify the seed, thus stimulating it to germinate.

3

Knobcone is still a different case. Although this tree may begin to produce fertile seed by the time it is ten years old, the seeds are kept sealed in the clusters of four-inch-long cones which cling to the trunk. Since the stout cones hang on the tree almost indefinitely, the bole often expands around and engulfs them over the decades.

The cone scales are sealed shut with resin and they open allowing the seed to fall only when the seal is melted by the heat of a fire. So, shortly after fire has swept through and destroyed a stand of knobcones, killing competing vegetation and leaving a seedbed of mineral soil, seeds drift down from the burned trees. Soon a new stand of knobcones will appear. Seeds of this tree show a high rate of germination, regardless of age.

knobcone pine
Pinus attenuata

singleleaf pinyon

Pinus monophylla
Pine family (*Pinaceae*)

Small, rounded nut pine of the arid Great Basin.

For thousands of years pinyon pines (also spelled piñon) have provided an essential food crop for residents of the American Southwest. Navajos and other peoples of the Colorado and Upper Rio Grande Basins relied heavily upon the nutritious seeds of Colorado pinyon, *Pinus edulis.* Westward in the Great Basin of Nevada and eastern California (a giant sink from which no river flows) Indians harvested the plump, half-inch-long seeds (1200/lb.) of singleleaf pinyon. Pinyon nuts are still gathered and used by some tribes, and large quantities harvested commercially are sold to tourists who can relive their summer travels while cracking and eating these tasty pine fruits around the fireplace at home.

Like Digger and knobcone pines, pinyons are small gray trees that grow on hot, dry mountain slopes below the limit of the conifer forest. However, that is about the extent of their similarity. *Singleleaf pinyon forms a broad belt of natural pine-nut orchards from about 5000 to 7500 feet elevation along the eastern skirts of the Sierra in the Owens Valley and Mono Basin. Farther east, this squatty pine colonizes most of the desert ranges of Nevada. It is that state's most abundant tree, and along with juniper, is the only tree present on many of the arid mountain ranges. Singleleaf pinyon can eke out an existence in high desert sites where annual precipitation is a scant 10 inches.*

The tree inhabits the west slopes of the Sierra only in a few localities. The northernmost grove is found in Yosemite National Park and consists of about 100 trees growing on a granite ridge between Tiltill Valley and Rancheria Creek overlooking Hetch Hetchy Reservoir. More pinyons can be seen clinging to the hot, south-facing wall of Kings Canyon above Cedar Grove. Indians from these areas on the Sierra west slope climbed across the Sierra crest in order to trade with Great Basin Piutes for obsidian to make arrowheads. It seems likely that these traders brought pinyon nuts back home across the mountains, and perhaps, intentionally or not, planted the pinyons of Yosemite and Kings Canyon.

Many amateur botanists first encountering this tree are surprised to learn that it is a pine, since pines are distinguished from other conifers by bearing needles in clusters of two to five. This pinyon is the only exception in the western hemisphere. Like other pines, the base of its needle cluster is wrapped in a papery sheath; but only a single short, stout, sharp-pointed needle is enclosed in each sheath. This single needle is apparently composed of 5 needles fused together, since 5 vascular bundles may be seen in its cross-section.

Still, it is the small, misshapen cone of this pinyon that is so important to squirrels, jays, humans, and other animals. Since pinyons form a squatty tree the Indian braves could easily knock down the cones with long poles. Squaws and children gleefully gathered up dozens of bushels of cones as they tumbled onto the dusty ground.

John Muir described how the families assembled around roasting fires in the evening, "in gay circles garrulous as jays," while they launched the first pine-nut feast of the season.

Seeds were sun parched to preserve them; squaws cracked the seed shells by rolling a stone pestle lightly over them. The kernels were eaten dried or roasted with no additional preparation.

Indians and whites also made other uses of singleleaf pinyon. The gum, or resin, which drips from cuts on the tree was collected and used by the Indians to soothe a sore throat, or put into a potion as a cure for rheumatism, tuberculosis, etc. Settlers made charcoal, cordwood, fencing, and timbers from this hardy desert tree.

singleleaf pinyon
Pinus monophylla

ponderosa pine

Pinus ponderosa
Pine family (*Pinaceae*)

Large, orange-barked pine inhabiting sunny canyons and lower mountain slopes throughout the West.

Ponderosa or "western yellow pine" is a tall, stately, open-growing evergreen that seems to represent the unconquered spirit and wide-open country known as the American West. Ponderosa grows on sunny mountainsides in every western state, southern British Columbia, northern Mexico, and also extends eastward as far as central Nebraska.

Park-like stands and open savannas of spreading yellow pines flow down the skirts of many a western mountain range to merge with the sagebrush and bunchgrass prairies below. In general, ponderosa forms the leading edge of the coniferous forest because it is more drought-resistant than other forest trees.

These towering pines were named "ponderosa" (from "ponderous") because of their great size by the early botanical explorer David Douglas. They form vast forests in sunny eastern Oregon, giving way to sagebrush prairie where the annual precipitation drops to under 12 inches. On the west slope of the Sierra Nevada annual rainfall may not be as much a limiting factor as is the length and severity of the summer drought.

In the Mother Lode country east of Sacramento ponderosas loom out above the chaparral on slopes as low as 2000 feet in elevation. Southward, in the vicinity of Sequoia National Park the traveler first encounters yellow pine, welcome outlyer of the cool conifer forest, nearer the 4500 or 5000 foot mark. Higher up the mountainsides, among the sugar pines and giant sequoias, shafts of sunlight glint off the orange, platy boles of ponderosa; but even in the southern Sierra "sun-loving" ponderosa generally reaches its upper limits at the comparatively modest elevation of 7000 feet. Yellow pines found scattered on southern exposures still higher up are stunted by repeated frost damage to their growth shoots.

Perhaps severe frosts on the Great Basin slope of the Sierra are responsible for ponderosa's very limited occurrence there. Ponderosa does not inhabit most of the cold high-desert country of Nevada, eastern Idaho, and western Wyoming, quite possibly because sites that are moist enough for it are too frosty in June and September. This conifer is best adapted to habitats having longer summers; as is the case with most mountain conifers, temperatures of -40 or even -50°F. in midwinter, when the tree is dormant, have little effect on ponderosa.

Ponderosa's ability to prosper on hot, arid sites is probably explained by its vigorous root growth. In one study of this species on dry sites, year-old seedlings grew to only three inches in height but, astonishingly, they developed taproots

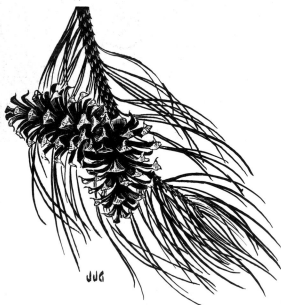

nearly two feet long! Four-year-olds averaged a foot in height but had sunk their roots five feet into the parched earth. Just a few tufts of leaves supplied moisture by an extensive root system. Perhaps because of this extensive root growth, gardeners find it difficult to successfully transplant yellow pine saplings.

In moister sites ponderosa is joined by a host of other conifers, such as sugar pine, Douglas-fir, incense-cedar, and white fir. All of these are better able to reproduce under forest shade than is yellow pine; consequently unless the forest is opened up by fire, windstorm, logging, etc. other confers will gradually grow up beneath and replace ponderosa. Before the twentieth century, lightning-caused and perhaps Indian-caused fires swept through the towering pine forests of the Sierra, killing encroaching brush and young incense-cedar and fir. Indians set fires in Yosemite Valley and elsewhere to help maintain open pine stands which offered vigorous grass and shrub forage for wildlife.

Thick-barked big ponderosas are highly resistant to burning. Fire scars can readily be seen at the base of old ponderosas in most stands throughout the West. In the past several years foresters have come to recognize the essential role of fire in maintaining natural forests. Most lightning fires are now allowed to run their natural course in the high country of Sequoia-Kings Canyon and Yosemite National Parks. Controlled fire is being employed to remove dense under-growth and to restore the vistas and open forests

ponderosa pine
Pinus ponderosa

that characterized Yosemite Valley a century ago.

Ponderosas are often venerable trees, and under natural conditions some may well have survived 20 or 30 fires. Like many other western conifers, yellow pines attain their greatest size under the sunny-summer, moist-snowy-winter climate on the western slope of the Sierra. For example, two large ponderosas along the Kings River trails above Cedar Grove are over 6½ feet in diameter, stand about 200 feet tall, and have survived roughly 600 years.

John Muir first described a yellow pine in Yosemite Valley that was larger than any known to be living today. This great, spreading tree, with a trunk 8 feet thick and 210 feet tall, was a popular tourist attraction. It died in the 1930's, but the huge fallen trunk still remains at Yellow Pine Beach below Sentinel Rock.

Another famous ponderosa overlooks that dead giant, and although it is about 80 feet tall and in very plain sight it is difficult to see from anyplace without binoculars. It grows on a narrow ledge a third of the way up the sheer granite wall of El Capitan. This cliff dweller gives testimony that many conifers do not require "soil"; these sturdy trees have roots that can find enough moisture and nutrients among narrow cracks in bedrock. It was not until 1955 when some rock climbers managed to scale their way up to this tree that its identity as ponderosa, rather than Jeffrey pine, was determined.

Jeffrey pine

Pinus jeffreyi
Pine family (*Pinaceae*)

Big, reddish-barked California mountain pine.

On first examination Jeffrey pine seems confusingly similar to ponderosa. Each species bears its luxuriant 8-10-inch-long needles in bundles of three, and together these two stalwart pines make up much of the sunny forest zone near the 6000-6500-foot level on the western slope of the Sierra. In areas where Jeffrey and ponderosa grow together, intermediate forms, which may be hybrids, sometimes add to the confusion. Still, people who observe and come to know Sierra trees will soon distinguish Jeffrey pine from ponderosa because of differences in their physical features and in the habitats in which they grow.

Jeffrey pine grows at mid-elevations, most commonly between 6000 and 9000 feet in the southern Sierra while ponderosa inhabits the lowest elevations of the conifer forest. Perhaps in response to the snowier, more rigorous winter conditions of its habitat, Jeffrey pine develops a stout trunk not so tall as ponderosa, but with a big-limbed, spreading crown. This is the rugged pine most often seen clinging to stark granite domes and gleaming rock slopes overlooking the major Sierra canyons. Having great resistance to frosty climates, *Jeffrey pine colonizes the entire length of the Sierra's jagged east escarpment above the high desert country.*

Jeffrey pine
Pinus jeffreyi

The cones and bark of Jeffrey pine distinguish it from ponderosa. Mature Jeffrey cones resemble a pineapple or a Digger pine cone in size and shape; they are usually 6 or 7 inches long and about 5 inches thick, while ponderosa cones measure about 4 by 3 inches. Jeffrey pine cones are made up of much thicker, firmer scales and the prickles or spines on the scales point down rather than sticking out as they do on ponderosa cones. This is one way to tell the two pines apart blindfolded; if you can grab a cone and pick it up without discomfort it is from Jeffrey pine. Another sightless identification is by sniffing furrows in the bark. Jeffrey pine bark has a vanilla-like odor, not usually present in ponderosa. Jeffrey pine bark is darker, reddish brown or pinkish, and appears much more furrowed than the ponderosa's, which is divided into large, light-colored plates.

Seeds of Jeffrey pine (4000/lb.) are three times as large as those of ponderosa, but still much smaller than singleleaf pinyon or Digger pine nuts. Jeffrey pine did, however, provide the Piute Indians with an epicurean delicacy. Caterpillars of the pandora moth eat Jeffrey pine needles, and the Great Basin Piutes in turn feasted upon the juicy caterpillars, known as "pe-agge". The Indians dug trenches among the pines and swept hordes of pe-agge into them in summer when masses of these two-to-three-inch-long larvae dropped from the trees. The caterpillars were roasted and mostly stored for future use. As much as a ton of pe-agge was taken in a season from a single harvest area. Modern Californians still harvest pe-agge for use in a "brittle" type candy.

In addition to providing excellent lumber, Jeffrey pine has supplied other important products for modern civilization. Ironically, this pine yielded an ingredient which helped develop the modern automobile, and the proliferation of automobiles is now largely responsible for destruction of thousands of acres of Jeffrey pine forest, in addition to that cleared to make highways and other roads.

The first intimation that Jeffrey pine contained a peculiar petroleum-based chemical came in 1867 when a turpentine distiller on Dogtown Ridge in Butte County unwittingly charged his still with pitch from Jeffrey pine rather than the usual ponderosa pitch. In the middle of the operation his still exploded. Later, a chemical called abietin was isolated in Jeffrey pine pitch. Abietin contains 96% normal heptane, a hydrocarbon also found in petroleum, and it was discovered that a purer and cheaper heptane could be produced from Jeffrey pine than by any other method. Heptane thus derived was used as a permanent and dependable "yardstick" for grading fuels under a system called "octane rating". This became a critical step in the evolution of internal combustion engines.

Nearly half a century later, in the early 1960's, experimental evidence implicated photochemical smog as the killer of ponderosa pines in the San Bernardino Mountains northeast of Los Angeles. Intensive studies made in 1970 by the U.S. Forest Service showed that over a million large Jeffrey and ponderosa pines in national forests north of the Los Angeles Basin were damaged or dying from this insidious brew of automobile exhaust and other waste gases.

sugar pine

Pinus lambertiana
Pine family (*Pinaceae*)

Massive California mountain pine with long, spreading branches and long pendant cones.

Sugar pine is the tallest, largest, and by most accounts the most magnificent of all the world's more than 100 species of pines. Its great reddish-brown trunks and towering crowns, made up of long limbs that stand out at right angles, dominate millions of acres of mountain forest from western Oregon to Baja California. *South of Alpine County sugar pine grows only on the western slope of the Sierra, under relatively moist conditions usually between 4500 and 7500 feet elevation.*

Old growth trees commonly stand 6 or 7 feet thick and 200 feet tall. The largest-known living pine measures 10 feet in diameter and 216 feet in height and was reported in 1967 growing in Tuolumne County. Yet even this forest giant would be dwarfed by the toppled sugar pine described by the Scotch botanist-explorer David Douglas in 1826.

Douglas hiked off alone that rainy October, heading south from Fort Vancouver on the Columbia River, up Oregon's Wilamette Valley. The local Indians watched him curiously as he wandered through the woods collecting plant specimens, and unlike other strangers not caring about trading or exploiting Nature's riches. They called him "The Man of Grass." Douglas had set out into unexplored territory in quest of the mysterious pines with huge cones of which the Indians had told him.

After 200 miles' walk Douglas came upon the great pines, largest of which was a tree 18 feet thick and 245 feet long which had blown over. Wanting to collect cones, he fired his gun at some hanging from the lofty branches; but the noise soon attracted eight hostile Indians.

Douglas made futile efforts to befriend them; and then resorted to cocking his gun and showing his determination to fight for his life. After several minutes of tense confrontation, the Indian leader gave sign that they wished for tobacco; Douglas signified that they could have it if they fetched a quantity of cones. Then as soon as they walked out of sight, he grabbed his three cones and some twigs and lit out in retreat from the sugar pine forest.

Sugar pine cones average a foot in length exclusive of the heavy stalk. They dangle like Christmas ornaments from the tips of palm-like upper limbs that reach out as much as 40 feet from the trunk. While still green the cones weigh up to 4 pounds, and since they often hang 150 feet up, it is wise to be alert when the squirrels are felling cones from treetops overhead!

As is the case with all conifers, sugar pine's seed-bearing cones develop from the tree's female "flowers"; male "flowers" form tiny pollen-bearing cones located at the tips of branches. During their second summer the female cones mature, their scales dry and open and the plump seeds fall onto the forest floor.

Squirrels shortcut the process by harvesting green cones of the various Sierran pines and ripping off scales to get the nuts. They bury some of these and retrieve only a small proportion of their caches, so they inadvertently plant millions of clusters of pine seeds. These in turn give rise to clusters of as many as 50 tiny pines which can be found emerging from the forest floor each summer whether they be from Digger pine caches at 2000 feet elevation or foxtail pine seed stores above 10,000 feet.

Sugar pine nuts (2100/lb.) about the size of a grain of corn are borne in pockets at the base of each cone scale. They were harvested by the Indians. The sugary resin, namesake of the tree, was considered a delicacy to the native Americans; John Muir wrote that he liked it better than maple sugar. It exudes from wounds on the trunk and crystallizes into candy-like kernels; but when eaten in quantity this sugar acts as a laxative. Indians used pitch from sugar pine to repair canoes and to fasten arrowheads and feathers to shafts.

Sugar pine bears slender, bluish-green needles five in a cluster. About three inches long, this foliage resembles that of western white pine (*Pinus monticola*). The latter, however, generally grows above 8000 feet elevation in the southern Sierra, while sugar pine rarely extends that high. Sugar pine cones are much larger and stouter, and

1 year old cone grows along with older cones

the branches reach out in contrast to western white pine's upturned upper boughs. Both trees, along with the timberline dweller white-bark pine, are classified as "white pines," and all three are threatened by the dreaded white-pine blister rust discussed in the next section. Although sugar pine is highly susceptible to this introduced disease, blister rust seems to find the droughty climate of the southern Sierra rather inhospitable and has caused limited damage here.

Like western white pine, sugar pine is unusual among western pines in being somewhat tolerant of shade. That is, it can reproduce successfully under a moderately heavy forest canopy — though not so successfully as white fir and incense-cedar. Its thick bark withstands fire, and sugar pines frequently attain ages of 500 years. White man has been the only real threat to the survival of these grand old trees.

The ingenious Yankees who flocked to California in the mid-1800's were quick to discover that these lofty pines yielded copious volumes of superb, even-grained, clear wood that worked well, did not warp or twist, and resisted rot. When the influx of settlers brought demand for house timbers and shingles, sugar pine was the answer.

John Sutter's famous mill at Coloma, where gold was discovered in 1848, was set up to cut sugar pine. In decades that followed, hordes of shake makers descended upon the sugar pine forest, and sawmills followed. Giant trees were plundered on thousands of acres of unprotected government land. Often only the finest wood was used, and less-than-perfect logs were left where they had been toppled. It was not until the national parks and national forests were created in the Sierra around the turn of the century that vestiges of the great forests of sugar pine were at last granted protection.

sugar pine
Pinus lambertiana

western white pine

Pinus monticola
Pine family (*Pinaceae*)

Silvery-colored pine of the moist high-country forest.

Western white pine brings a flavor of Idaho and some of New England to the High Sierra. Eastern white pine (*Pinus strobus*), a similar and closely related tree, provided the finest softwood timber in the American Colonies; the English monarchy even marked certain prime specimens with a broad arrow to reserve them for masts for the Royal Navy. "White pine" lured early lumbermen across the forests of the Northeastern United States, and then into the moist and snowy mountains of northern Idaho. Fortunately the era of Conservation — in which Teddy Roosevelt, Gifford Pinchot, and John Muir figured prominently — intervened and great forest reserves were established before the West, too, was denuded.

In the Pacific Northwest white pine grows as low as sea level. *By contrast, in the Sierra it finds a suitably humid environment only at high elevations, usually 7500-10,500 feet,* and perhaps because of the short growing season and exposure to high winds, it grows squatty, seldom exceeding 100 feet in height. Still, like their 150-200-foot-tall Idaho kin, Sierra white pines develop strikingly beautiful five-foot-thick trunks encased in black-ish bark which is deeply fissured into a checkerboard pattern. Also, western white pines from both regions produce distinctive upper limbs which sweep upward like arms reaching into the heavens. Long (6-12") slender cones hang from these silvery-colored boughs; before they dry out and expand, their appearance serves as inspiration for the common name "finger-cone pine."

In the Sierra this tree is sometimes called "little sugar pine." Although it occupies the eastern slope of the Sierra southward past Mammoth Lakes, white pine is more abundant along the moister, western slope; here it spreads southward to the end of the high country in southern Kern County.

Magnificent spreading western white pines can be seen at many locations in the central and southern Sierra, including the highway pass on Mount Rose (northeast of Lake Tahoe), Sonora Pass, Tioga Pass, and at Lodgepole Campground in Sequoia National Park. Miles of Sierra hiking trails lead through stands sprinkled with great old white pines. One giant growing west of Porcupine Flat near the Tioga Road in Yosemite has the largest girth of any western white pine known; it stands eight feet thick above the butt swell and 120 feet tall.

Because of their gnarled, limby forms, Sierra white pines would not provide choice lumber like their Pacific Northwest counterparts. The wood from the latter is largely clear and smooth, seemingly without grain. It is prized for window and door frames and moldings, and is the wood in wooden matches and toothpicks. White pine works so easily that it makes a splendid whittling wood; lengths of chain (composed of interlocking links) are among intricate items often fashioned from it.

Unfortunately white pine timber is

being depleted rapidly as a result of a fungus which man accidentally brought over from Europe in the early 1900's. This blister rust is deadly to white pine, in the same sense that chestnut blight, Dutch elm disease, and the gypsy moth are deadly to certain eastern hardwoods. In each case modern man unwittingly upset the ecological applecart by importing a foreign tree pest to which our trees had acquired no natural resistance.

When blister rust spread into the stronghold of white pine in northern Idaho in the 1930's a multimillion dollar program to save the trees was launched by the federal government. During three decades that followed, thousands of men were hired to grub out currant and gooseberry bushes from British Columbia to the central Sierra. By thus destroying the alternate host necessary to the completion of blister rust's life-cycle, foresters hoped to save western white pine and sugar pine.

However, the rust spores can be carried ten or more miles by winds to infect new trees, provided moisture is adequate. In most areas the currant-eradication program proved futile as did a later chemical attack on the rust. Now efforts are largely concentrated upon cross-breeding the few naturally resistant white pines in order to obtain large quantities of rust-resistant stock for planting; this program is promising largely because it seeks to enhance and speed up Nature's own approach — the slow evolutionary process of building up a resistant strain, generation by generation.

western white pine
Pinus monticola

lodgepole pine

Pinus contorta
var. *murrayana*
Pine family (*Pinaceae*)

A small slender pine that clothes the high Western mountains in dense forests.

The name "lodgepole pine" was reputedly coined as a result of the Lewis and Clark Expedition of 1804-1806. The explorers found that Indians from the upper Great Plains journeyed into the Rocky Mountains to cut the straight, slender trunks of these trees for constructing lodges or tepees. It may seem contradictory that lodgepole's technical name means "contorted pine"; but that epithet is appropriate for the Pacific Coast tideland form of this species, which is a twisted little tree commonly known as "shore pine." Inland varieties grow like "lodgepoles" in crowded stands that cover large tracts of high country in the Cascade, Sierra Nevada, and Rocky Mountains as well as the boreal forest and soggy muskeg of western Canada. In the Sierra this species has several different growth forms, ranging from large spreading trees in meadowy or protected sites to shrubby forms at timberline.

Like the deciduous conifer known as eastern larch or tamarack (*Larix laricina*), lodgepole pine is a small tree often growing in wet meadows or bogs. Perhaps because of this superficial similarity, in the Sierra where there are no tamaracks lodgepole pine has often erroneously been dubbed "tamarack." John Muir referred to lodgepole as "tamarack pine," and the many "Tamarack Lakes," etc. in the Sierra attest to the abundance of lodgepole.

Lodgepole occupies both slopes of the Sierra between about 6500 and 10,500 feet in our region, but it often extends much lower along watercourses. For instance, it grows along the Merced River in Yosemite Valley at only 4000 feet elevation.

Lodgepole is easily distinguished from other Sierra trees since it is the only one bearing needles in groups of two. The needles are also unusually stout and rather short for a Sierra pine, being about two inches in length. The rounded cones are shorter still, and are the smallest among those of western pines. Since lodgepole pine cones are armed with sharp prickles, and because they cover much of the ground in the High Sierra, it behooves campers to carefully brush them aside before spreading out a sleeping bag or air mattress!

Lodgepole is a precocious and prolific cone-bearer, usually yielding some fruit by about ten years of age. Often the cones hang on trees for decades; thus some trees appear loaded with thousands of burs. The trunk may grow out around and eventually engulf cones attached to it, so that boards cut from such trees have cones imbedded in them.

Outside of California a lodgepole 20 inches thick is considered exceptionally large, while trees attain three foot diameters rather frequently in the Sierra, and the record-sized lodgepole growing on the Stanislaus National Forest measures 6½ feet through. But perhaps more remarkable are the facts that in the High Sierra lodgepole often reaches timberline and that at higher elevations and perhaps in moist basins as well, it seems to be a "climax" species — able to reproduce and remain dominant in the forest for centuries. In contrast to this situation, in most regions lodgepole depends upon fire or other disturbance to periodically destroy the forest; otherwise it will be shaded out by firs and other shade-tolerant species.

One might conclude that extensive forests of sun-bleached lodgepole snags seen in the Sierra are caused by wildfire. Actually the "ghost forests" lining the Tioga Road and many trails are caused by the needle-miner moth. The larvae of this insect obtain food and shelter hollowing out the needles of lodgepole pine, and outbreaks of needle-miner have defoliated and killed sizeable tracts of lodgepole forest. Because this insect is a natural predator on lodgepole (moth and tree having co-existed for millenniums) there is no danger that the tree would be largely wiped out as is the case with chestnut blight or white pine blister rust and their hosts. Thus, needle-miner is generally allowed to run its natural course in National Parks and National Forest Wilderness.

Chemical controls have been used with only marginal success; more recently the emphasis on protecting lodgepole in the commercial timberlands of the Sierra has shifted toward natural con-

lodgepole pine
Pinus contorta var. murrayana

trols. Chemical controls temporarily reduced populations of needle-miner, but also abetted the surviving moths by ridding them of some of their more than two dozen species of natural parasites! A biological control might instead be aimed at improving conditions for the moth's most effective parasites.

The work of mountain pine beetles, which appears as a pattern of grooves etched on the surface of whitened snags, can also be observed readily in Sierra lodgepole forests. Unlike many other insects and unlike diseases these beetles generally kill only large, healthy trees. The beetles lay eggs in the bark and their larvae tunnel around eating the sap layer and girdling the tree in the process. Smaller trees are seldom affected since their sap layer is too thin to provide suitable habitat for the over-wintering larvae.

whitebark pine
Pinus albicaulis

whitebark pine

Pinus albicaulis
Pine family (*Pinaceae*)

Short, spreading tree or wind-scoured and pruned shrub of timberline in the Pacific Coast States and Northern Rockies.

Although whitebark pine is often an "old friend" to hikers and mountain climbers, most auto-oriented visitors never see it. Not that whitebark is scarce, either. It is distributed widely in mountain ranges from central British Columbia and Alberta southward to Wyoming and to the southern end of the High Sierra; but throughout this broad domain whitebark grows only high in the mountains, near timberline.

In the south-central Sierra, whitebark can be found between 10,000 and 12,000 feet. Its lower limits are reached by the few roads crossing the Sierra Crest—at Sonora Pass, Tioga Pass, and Minaret Summit. By contrast, a sizeable proportion of the hundreds of miles of trails in the High Sierra thread their way across an awesome granite landscape sprinkled with whitebark pines.

Whitebark can eke out an existence on exposed southerly slopes at and above the limits of other tree species. It takes on a variety of growth forms including single-trunk stout trees in high basins and stunted multi-stemmed trees on exposed slopes. Also, it grows as tiny wind-pruned shrubs huddled in the lee of rocks high up in the tundra zone; the crown of such conifer cushions is composed of hundreds of tiny branchlets that meet in a perfect hedge surface. The gardener that each year shears off protruding shoots is the winter wind. Relentless blizzards blast the twigs with grains of ice and sand, and winds dry out any exposed green shoots while the gound is frozen and water for transpiration is unavailable. John Muir counted annual growth-rings on some of these shrublike whitebark pines, finding one to be, ". . . 426 years old, whose trunk is only six inches in diameter; and one of its supple branchlets, hardly an eighth of an inch in diameter inside the bark, is seventy-five years old, and so filled with oily balsam, and so well seasoned by storms, that we may tie it in knots like whip-cord."

Although whitebark is rarely logged in any region, it is of considerable aesthetic appeal to humans and provides essential food for the native inhabitants of the high-country. The dense bushy growth of whitebark pine shelters campers from biting winds. Likewise, some of the Sierra's plump blue grouse roost in thick crowns of whitebark and foxtail pines protected from gales and unseen by marauding goshawks or hunting humans while they subsist on a diet of needles and buds from their piney homes.

Chickarees, chipmunks, and the raucous black, white, and gray jays known as Clark's nutcrackers seem to regard whitebark as the pinyon of timberline. In late summer and early fall the otherwise serene whitebark groves ring with the activity of the nut harvest. Chicka-rees scold and chatter as they fell the purple cones and scamper across rocky ground to cache them. Clark's nutcrakers issue harsh "kr-a-a-a's!" and hammer through thick cone scales to get at the rich seeds (3600/lb.). Thus, most of the frequently ample whitebark cone crop is harvested by residents year after year. In some areas even black bears get involved through sniffing out and raiding of the squirrels' cone caches.

Like other high-country dwellers — limber, foxtail, and western white pines — whitebark bears its yellow-green needles in clusters of five. These average about two inches long. By comparison, western white

Eaten by squirrels

Eaten by Clark's nutcracker

pine needles are longer, more slender, and have a bluish cast; foxtail pine needles are much shorter and they clothe twigs in a manner resembling a fox tail. Moreover, cones, bark, and growth-form are so different that whitebark pine would seldom be confused with anything except limber pine.

Needles and twigs of whitebark and limber pines are almost identical. Despite their likeness, a person who knows what to look for can usually tell whitebark from limber pine in the field without difficulty. White-bark's unusual cone provides the clue. It is purple, thick-scaled, and it disintegrates when seeds are ripe, leaving only a 2-3-inch-long spin-dle-like core attached to the upper boughs. Limber pine has huskier 4-5-inch-long cones that turn from green to light brown when ripening. Then the scales spread, nuts fall out, and as with other pines the spent cones remain intact on the tree and on the ground for a few years after they fall.

In late summer or early fall new cones of both species can be seen in the crowns and identified by color and size. At other times a quick search of the ground beneath trees is revealing. Old cones from previous seasons should not be hard to find under a limber pine. If no cones appear, whitebark is the likely suspect; confirmation is made by finding old cone cores attached to upper limbs or loose scales and cores of disintegrated cones on the ground. The two species seldom grow together in extensive mixtures since they seem to be largely restricted to somewhat different habitats, as is discussed further under limber pine.

limber pine

Pinus flexilis
Pine family (*Pinaceae*)

Spreading or sprawling tree of high windy ridges and dry slopes in the interior of the American West.

Both the common and scientific names of this tree describe the trait that adapts it to survival in the windiest parts of the West. Limber pine forms a stout, squatty tree well anchored to steep rocky ridges by a sturdy taproot; the boughs sweep out and up and the foliage is borne on twigs so supple they can be tied into knots without breaking!

Unlike the closely-related whitebark pine, which is largely restricted to the snowy timberline zone, limber pine characteristically occupies dry rocky, windy southern exposures in a variety of forest zones. In Alberta and Montana it often forms the "lower timberline" growing on the skirts of the Rockies where inadequate moisture causes the forest to give way to bunchgrass prairie. Southward, limber pine is one of few trees inhabiting the arid mountain ranges of the Great Basin.

In the southern portion of its distribution, from the east slope of the Sierra Nevada to Colorado, limber pine grows in scattered stands from the middle forest zones up to timberline, between 8000 and 12,000 feet. Near its upper limits the trunks often arch over like a crescent so the treetop touches ground as a result of centuries of

limber pine
Pinus flexilis

mis-shaping and flailing by the stinging winds. Sometimes a trunk more than a foot thick grows straight out along the ground surface instead of into the air. Some of the trees in desert ranges especially, become gnarled and venerable.

Whitebark pine forms stands in cold, snowy sites where the growing season (about two months long) is too short to allow other conifers to provide much competition. Similarly, limber pine occupies much of its habitat by default; although other pines, fir, or spruce may be superior competitors for moisture, nutrients, and growing room in ordinary sites, they can barely survive in dry, windy limber pine sites. Limber pine dominates the entire forest belt (albeit a narrow one) on some of the arid mountains in Nevada.

Most of the Sierra Nevada is apparently too snowy and moist to provide habitat for limber pine. *Still, the species is fairly well-represented along the dry east escarpment of the range southward from Mono Pass in Yosemite* *National Park. Spreading limber pines with upswept limbs grow on boulder-strewn slopes and ridges near roadheads at Whitney Portal, above Glacier Lodge, and at Onion Valley, where both limber and whitebark pines shade the picnic tables.* Limber pine is the only associate of the 4000-year-old bristlecone pines which grow at 10,000-11,000 feet in the White Mountains immediately east of the Sierra.

Bristlecone is very similar to the foxtail pine of the southern High Sierra. Limber and foxtail pines grow together along the upper east slopes, near the crest of the Sierra, and a striking example of their different growth habits can be seen between 10,700 and 11,000 feet elevation along the John Muir Trail above Whitney Portal. Under the harsh growing conditions limber pines form huge prostrate shrubs, sprawling across exposed granite bedrock, while even at the very limit of conifers, foxtail pines seem defiant of the wind, ice and snow as they grow straight and 20-40 feet tall. This species is our next subject.

foxtail pine

Pinus balfouriana
Pine family (*Pinaceae*)

Stout and durable tree of the highest peaks in the southern Sierra.

While the giant sequoias are the indisputable monarchs of the temperate Sierra forest, another tree, colossal in its own way, clings to life high up on the steep, windswept granite ridges at timberline. The harsh climate with its two-month growing season and summer drought coupled with almost non-existent "soil," stunts the vegetation. Near 11,000 feet all tree species except this one conifer are reduced to the sprawling many-stemmed shrubs and cushions known as "krummholz," German for "crooked wood." But, despite the fierce conditions, foxtail pine always grows erect, usually producing a single stout trunk.

An excellent place to see foxtail pine is along the high trails leading out of Mineral King in Sequoia National Forest. The largest-known foxtail, 8½ feet thick and 70 feet tall, can be found on the southwest-facing slope immediately east of Timber Gap at about 10,000 feet. *The splendid stand of foxtails on Alta Peak in Sequoia National Park is one of the more accessible sites in foxtail country since it can be reached on a long day-hike.* Impressive western white pines five feet thick grow at around 10,000 feet; but they do not match the biggest foxtail pines which dwell still higher up, where growing conditions are more adverse, exposure and drought more intense.

A remarkable foxtail over 6½ feet thick and 60 feet tall inhabits the southwest facing slope near the Alta Peak trail at 10,500 feet. Like many other foxtails, this veteran is only half-alive. Nearly all of its original trunk eventually succumbed to the ice-blasting blizzards. Then a large branch on the leeward or upslope side bent upward to form a new trunk; but after another century or two, the gales and hurricanes killed this too. Later, a branch on the second trunk grew erect to form a third trunk; so this "double piggy-back" tree continues its battle to survive. Fifty feet in the air, the third trunk, too, is dying on the windward side, and a large branch on its sheltered side seems destined to take on the role of trunk number four. Increment borings (pencil-sized drill cores of wood) taken from this tree and five other large foxtails indicate by their annual growth rings that they are probably in the neighborhood of 1000 years old.

Like many other timberline trees, foxtail pine exhibits incredible vitality. High-altitude species have been naturally selected over millions of years to achieve this hardiness. One sentinel (4½ feet thick and 45 feet tall) growing in the stand on Alta Peak has just a little clump of living branches remaining half-way up on its sheltered side. This remnant of surviving foliage receives its nourishment through a narrow strip of bark covering only 10-15% of the trunk's circumference. Otherwise this large tree is a whitened, weather-polished snag. Another straw-colored foxtail snag at 10,800 feet near Sphinx Lakes in Kings Canyon National Park has two living branches, one on either side of the trunk, and each nourished by

a separate strip of cambial (bark) tissue several inches wide.

Still another big foxtail on Alta Peak has a similarly slender life-line of bark clinging to its weathered bole; but that strip was finally eroded through and now the tree is dead. Foxtails, however, endure in many different forms. Up the mountain from these living snags, in an equally exposed position, grows a tree 5½ feet thick and 50 feet tall that has a dense, luxuriant growth and an unscathed trunk.

Even more amazing than these foxtails is one found atop Silliman Ridge, also in Sequoia National Park. A dead, hollow stump about five feet thick has a narrow zone of sound wood extending upward and a thin ribbon of bark cemented to this. This forms the 20-foot-long shred of life that supports two stout limbs which bear an ample crop of needles and cones. Yet, a man can easily climb inside the vacant stump to observe its state of utter decay.

After perhaps 1000 years, a foxtail pine will have at last been totally killed by the elements. Disease does not seem to play a critical part in the death of such trees, probably because disease and decay organisms are hampered by the cold climate. Charred remains of lightning-struck foxtails lie strewn about in the high-country. The resinous, dry wood of these weathered trees burns intensely hot and apparently a veteran pine struck by lightning may quickly become an arborescent torch. There is probably little chance of a huge conflagration spreading through the foxtail forests, however, since these pines normally grow 30-60 feet or more apart in wide-open stands. Also, the "forest floor" here consists largely of non-combustible mineral earth and rocks.

These drought-resistant trees have deep, spreading root systems. Like shrubs in the desert, foxtails must have plenty of rooting room in which to obtain adequate moisture from their well-drained rocky sites during dry summers. The foxtail's only important and dependable source of water is meltwater from the heavy snowpack — which lingers into July in most stands.

In the Sierra, foxtail inhabits only the southern high-country, mostly within Sequoia and Kings Canyon National Parks, and there it is often abundant. However, foxtail also grows in several scattered patches atop the northern California Coast Ranges (Salmon, Scott, and Yolla Bolly Mountains), more than 300 airline miles to the northwest. There is no apparent reason why foxtail does not occur farther north in the Sierra. Once it probably was more widespread, and then later much of its range was inundated by the massive Ice Age glaciers. But why would the icecaps have wiped out foxtail pine in the central and not the southern Sierra? Apparently there was a refuge from ice and perpetual snow in the south, and foxtail has slowly migrated back northward; but then why couldn't it have returned more quickly like other timberline pines? Like the giant sequoia, foxtail pine grows as a native only in California.

Sierra foxtails seldom extend much below 10,000 feet. One of the lowest known is a spire-like tree growing in the open along the east side of the dirt road up Mineral King Valley, about half a mile south of the Sawtooth Pass-Timber Gap trailhead. Others can be seen near the roadhead in Onion Valley above Independence. In such sheltered sites foxtails stand out among other conifers because of their taller spire-shaped crowns. The distinctive foliage consists of inch-long clusters of five needles which clothe branchlets in a manner resembling a fox tail, largely because a given year's new crop of needles may persist through 17 years — much longer than leaves of other evergreens.

foxtail pine
Pinus balfouriana

white fir

Abies concolor
Pine family (*Pinaceae*)

A tall fir on moist mid-elevation mountainsides throughout the Pacific Southwest

White fir and red fir are the only true or "balsam" firs inhabiting the Sierra. True firs are unique among North American conifers in bearing their cones erect in the uppermost boughs. These barrel-shaped cones perched upright in the pointed tree tops are often frosted with white pitch that sparkles in the sunlight.

Chickarees cut these little seed-barrels down and stash them away for winter food. Cones they miss disintegrate on the tree in autumn, the scales and seeds dropping and drifting down onto thick duff on the forest floor. For this reason whole fir cones can only be found on the ground when felled by squirrels or windstorms. Foresters who collect cones to obtain ripe seed for planting follow the hyperactive squirrels and use some of their cone caches.

In addition to eating seeds of white fir, chickarees frequently make their nests in the bushy crowns or in hollow rotten spots high up in the trunk. Deer browse on the foliage of young white firs, giving them a hedged appearance. Bears hibernate in the cavities found in the base of big old white firs; in fact most of the bear dens known in Yosemite National Park are situated in hollow trunks of white and red firs. Human hikers, too, prefer the ground around the bases of large

white firs for camping, although of course old, rotting trees can be hazardous. The flattened, sweeping boughs of mature trees are Nature's own umbrella tent. The area beneath such trees remains dry even after consecutive days of rainy weather.

Thus there is a very practical value in being able to distinguish white fir from other trees. The foliage is familiar to most people since white fir is probably the most common Christmas tree in California. Douglas-fir and red fir also bear their needles singly. Douglas-fir needles, however, differ from those of true firs in being sharp-pointed rather than blunt (although cone-bearing upper branches of true firs do have sharp needles), and the distinctive Douglas-fir cones can usually be found all over the ground, since they do not disintegrate when ripe.

White fir has long, pale bluish-green or gray-green needles. On lower branches of vigorous trees these needles measure two or sometimes three inches in length — longer than other firs in North America. The luxuriant foliage and regular, pyramidal shape of young white firs makes them a favorite for planting in gardens and lawns. Both the common and technical names denote the whitish or gray cast of the tree; in addition to this color of foliage, the bark on young trees is silvery, taking on an ashen hue and becoming deeply furrowed with age. In contrast, needles of red fir are short (an inch or less); they clothe the branches more densely, and are dark blue-green. The bark on mature red firs is purplish and inner bark is bright red, while inner bark of white firs is yellow-brown.

True firs are known as balsams because the bark on young trees has blisters filled with a clear, aromatic pitch known as Canadian balsam. Balsam is used for mounting objects on microscope slides, in the manufacture of fine lacquers, and as a cement for lenses.

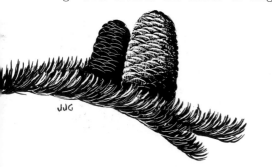

White fir occupies moist mountain slopes from southern Oregon to Baja California and eastward to Colorado and New Mexico. *In the central and southern Sierra it grows between 3500 and 7500 feet elevation and is common on both the western and eastern slopes of the range. Red fir grows generally at higher elevations.*

The "Christmas trees" growing beneath the towering giant sequoias are white firs. Seeds of this species are capable of germinating and growing in heavy accumulations of duff which hinder or stifle reproduction of pines and sequoias in these groves. But the densely-crowned fir is much more susceptible to death by wildfire than are pines and sequoia with their thick protective bark and long clear boles, so under natural conditions (with lightning fires) fir would seldom replace sequoias or the sunny pines over very much of the forest landscape. Moreover, freshly burned sites are apt to be readily taken over by vigorous young pines and sequoias that outstrip and over top white fir saplings in initial height growth.

Like so many trees inhabiting the western slope of the Sierra, white firs often become forest giants in their own right. Trees five feet thick and 150 feet tall are found rather commonly. Many white firs larger than

white fir
Abies concolor

this can be seen near the shores of Merced Lake in Yosemite National Park, and America's largest-known white fir, 8½ feet thick by 180 feet tall, stands in the mountains northwest of Pine Flat Reservoir in the Sierra National Forest.

Natural root grafting, a fusing of root systems from different trees, has been found often among white firs in the Sierra. This phenomenon can be detected above ground rather easily in areas where some of the firs have been cut. A doughnut-shaped callus of bark tissue often grows over the sawed-off stump indicating that the stump is joined by its root system to a still-living tree.

red fir

Abies magnifica
Pine family (*Pinaceae*)

Stately, symmetrical tree of the "snow forest" from high mountains of southwestern Oregon to the southern Sierra

Majestic red firs with their luxuriant bluish boughs and thick, furrowed, chocolate bark, revealing a tinge of purple in the shafts of sunlight, epitomize the deep-snow forest of the Sierra. Unlike most other forest trees in the Sierra, large red firs often grow close together in pure groves, their heavy crowns forming a somber canopy that keeps the forest floor shady, moist, and cool in August when most of California is sweltering.

The red fir zone of the southern Sierra covers cool exposures between about 6500 and 9000 feet, and in these serene forests even the summer visitor is apt to sense that mountain snows never release their hold for long. Varied ice crystals sift down silently, or blow down harshly, in major and minor storm periods from November until May, producing snowfalls that average 400-500 inches a winter. *As one might suspect, red fir occurs only sporadically on the drier eastern*

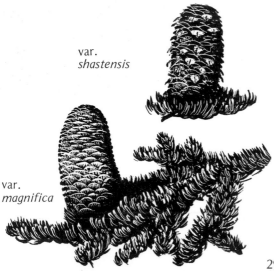

var.
shastensis

var.
magnifica

slope of the range south of Mammoth Lakes. It does grow in Lone Pine Canyon beneath the eastern wall of Mount Whitney.

Long after spring arrives in the sunny ponderosa and Jeffrey pine stands on southern exposures, the shadowy red fir forest stays like an ice-box, harboring last winter's snowpack on the dark forest floor. In fact, seeds from red fir can often be found germinating on the snowpack late in June; they root into the snow, but do not produce seed-leaves, and perish when at long last July's warmth reveals the ground.

The use of common names such as "red fir" often results in confusion because people in different localities are apt to use the same name for different species. For instance, West Coast loggers often refer to Douglas-fir as "red fir." Only the standardized common names published in the U. S. Forest Service *Check List of Trees of the United States* are used here; but anyone with more than a casual interest in the identity of forest trees is wise to become familiar with their scientific names.

In the case of our red fir such knowledge would clear up the relationship between the two types of red fir found in the Sierra. Commonly known as California red fir (*Abies magnifica* var. *magnifica*) and Shasta red fir (*Abies magnifica* var. *shastensis*), the scientific names show them to be varieties of the same species; thus one would expect them to be quite similar. Indeed they are. In fact the only known external difference is that Shasta red fir has tawny, papery bracts extending from between the scales of its barrel-shaped cones, while the purple cones of California red fir show no bracts. The Shasta variety predominates in Sequoia and Kings Canyon National Parks vicinity while California red fir is more abundant near Yosemite; but both types grow together and apparently hybridize, and differentiating between them seems to be largely of academic interest since the two trees are ecologically similar.

Red firs are grown commercially and marketed at a premium as "silvertip Christmas trees," because of their beautiful spire-like crowns composed of boughs richly-carpeted with blue-green needles. John Muir praised this luxuriant foliage as a mountaineer's mattress, "Two rows of the plushy branches overlapping along the middle, and a crescent of smaller plumes mixed with ferns and flowers for a pillow, form the very best bed imaginable . . . any combination of cloth, steel springs, and feathers seems vulgar in comparison." For better or worse, however, there are now too many campers sharing the Sierra to allow them to hack down red fir foliage for their beds or cut off living trees to make tent poles. Today such destruction of living plants is of necessity unlawful in national parks and forests.

As the symmetrical young trees mature, their crowns become rounded, and after being battered by winter storms for a century or two the veteran red firs appear picturesquely ragged or broken. Sierra loggers have dubbed old-growth red firs "widow makers" because trees that appear sound are often rotten or even hollow. Old red firs often crash down in only moderate windstorms, and compared to other Sierra conifers they seem rather short-lived. A gigantic tree growing at Glacier Point overlooking Yosemite Valley was seven feet thick and 186 feet tall,

red fir
Abies magnifica

but only 260 years old when it crashed to the ground in a storm.

The great old partially-rotten trees provide nesting sites for chickarees, flying squirrels, various woodpeckers, owls, and other wildlife, and the rich purplish-brown bark on snags and downed trees converts to splendid glowing coals in a campfire. Red fir bark provided the red-hot embers that used to be shoved off Glacier Point to create the 1000-foot "Firefall" viewed nightly by thousands of visitors far below in Yosemite Valley. However, this event has been discontinued because it was felt that such an artificial spectacle is inappropriate in a national park where the wonders enjoyed should be those so amply provided by Mother Nature.

Douglas-fir

Pseudotsuga menziesii
Pine family (*Pinaceae*)

A large, vigorous, adaptable tree inhabiting all forested regions of the West.

How ironic it seems that North America's most important timber tree, a species which grows from central Mexico almost to Alaska, is one whose botanical identity is obscure. It was first classified as a pine, and was given the common name, "Oregon pine." However, even casual inspection showed that this magnificent conifer did not bear needles in clusters like pines, nor did it have pine-like cones.

In fact, pine was one of few types of conifers that it did not resemble! The bark of young Douglas-fir is smooth and pocked with balsam blisters like the firs (*Abies*); the sharp inch-long needles resemble spruce (*Picea*) or yew (*Taxus*); and the cones look like chubby spruce cones except for unique three-pronged fork-like bracts that project from between the scales. John Muir called it "Douglas Spruce," and it was classified as a true fir and as a hemlock (*Tsuga*) in botanical literature in the 1800's.

Botanists returning from exploration in the Himalayas and mountains of China and Japan brought back samples of other trees like "Oregon pine," and in 1867 the technical name *Pseudotsuga*, meaning "false hemlock," was proposed for this singular group of trees.

The botanical name now acknowledges the original

Douglas-fir
Pseudotsuga menziesii

discoverer (the Scotch naturalist, Dr. Archibald Menzies) while the accepted common name, "Douglas-fir" (for David Douglas, who re-discovered it) is applied to all of the several members of the genus *Pseudotsuga* — two species of which grow in California. Hopefully, the nomenclature of this species is at last resolved, and this is why "Douglas-fir" (or "Douglasfir") cannot be correctly written as two words — the tree simply is not any kind of a "fir" (*Abies*).

Another species, *Pseudotsuga macrocarpa*, known as "bigcone Douglas-fir," which is a smaller tree bearing larger cones, inhabits the mountains of Southern California — the one area of the West where common Douglas-fir does not grow.

The distribution of Douglas-fir (*Pseudotsuga menziesii*) in the Sierra is quite interesting; but a little more background information on the tree may help in understanding its range here. This tree has two varieties — the Pacific Coast form and the Rocky Mountain form. Coastal Douglas-fir is the grand timber tree of the Northwest, and it extends southward into the central Sierra. This is the tree that sometimes attains heights of 300 feet and ranks second only to the California coastal redwood in being the world's tallest tree.

Although foliage and cones of Rocky Mountain Douglas-fir are similar to the coastal type, the two varieties must be very different genetically because the inland form is able to grow in much drier and colder habitates, where annual precipitation may average even less than 15 inches. The Rocky Mountain form probably could colonize the high, dry slopes of the southern Sierra; *however, only the Coastal form of Pseudotsuga menziesii occurs in California, and because it requires a moist, but not-too-cold environment, it becomes scarce southward in the Sierra.*

In the Yosemite region Douglas-fir is largely confined to the cool, moist canyons between 3500 and 5500 feet, where it is commonly found as a stout, corky-barked old tree with massive limbs, growing among boulders and perhaps framing the view of a waterfall. Even here at its southern range limit coastal Douglas-fir attains remarkable size. Two veterans growing near the roadhead at Mirror Lake, beneath the wall of Half Dome stand seven feet thick and close to 200 feet tall, and John Muir reported some even larger.

Such venerable giants have lived through many a forest fire, insulated from damage by corky bark up to one foot thick. In fact, natural fires help to perpetuate Douglas-fir. Surviving veterans spread viable seed over the burned areas. Experiments have shown that the light (42,000/lb.), winged seed is capable of traveling one-fourth mile from the parent tree in just a moderate breeze.

Although rather common at the foot of canyon walls in Yosemite Valley, Douglas-fir does not grow much farther south. The southernmost grove known is reported in the vicinity of Huntington Lake, Sierra National Forest. (Douglas-fir does not inhabit the Sierra's east slope in our region.) It seems likely, though, that other groves still farther south await discovery.

Douglas-fir can be distinguished from all other Sierra conifers by its three-inch-long cones covered with three-pronged bracts; these are often abundant hanging in the trees or on the ground. Buds at the end of branchlets provide another key; they look like chubby miniature cigars with a sharp point and are made up of dark-brown overlapping scales. In contrast, true fir buds are smaller, blunt, and waxy. The outer bark on mature Douglas-fir is also unique, and can even be used to identify stumps of trees that died 50 years ago. Cutting into the outer bark with a pocket knife reveals wavy bands of tan and dark brown, somewhat like the pattern in a pile of bacon slices.

mountain hemlock

Tsuga mertensiana
Pine family (*Pinaceae*)

Large handsome tree with luxuriant foliage found in snowy Pacific Coast mountains.

Mountain hemlock brings a flavor of the glacier-clad Alaskan coastal ranges to the Sierra Nevada. Along nearly 1000 miles of the mountainous Alaskan coast from Ketchikan past Seward and Anchorage, this tree dominates the forest from a few hundred feet above tidewater to timberline, frequently occurring near the 2000-foot level. Southward, mountain hemlock prospers in a similarly snowy, moist, and cool zone at 4000 to 6000 feet elevation in western Washington. Still farther south along the Cascades and Sierra Nevada the "Alaska-like" mountain hemlock habitat is generally confined to north-facing slopes at increasingly higher elevations. *This graceful mountain conifer reaches its southern limit in snowy basins of the southern Sierra at 9000 to 10,500 feet, often bordering meadows, icy streams, or cirque lakes.*

In his first book, *The Mountains of California* (1894), John Muir gives an eloquent 1000-word account of "the most singularly beautiful of all the California coniferae" — mountain hemlock. A large proportion of today's backpackers and mountaineers seems to agree with that assessment. From the ground up, mountain hemlock trunks are clothed luxuriantly in boughs of deep green and bluish-green foliage sprinkled with ornate purple cones; the tree's growing tip droops slightly as do the ends of upper branches.

As John Muir and others have observed, mountain hemlock seems to exhibit a sort of delicate grace even though it is in no way frail. At the same time, stout old hemlocks, with massive wind-battered crowns and sturdy boles clad in dark, furrowed bark seem to have a rugged air. In any case the tree's form and lush foliage befits its moist Alaska-like habitat.

At the limit of trees, mountain hemlock may grow as a huge, sprawling shrub with so many upturned branch-trunks that one tree appears to form a small grove. Patches of slender pole-size hemlocks occupy snowdrift sites where they are flattened each winter by the burden of snow and ice that piles up on their crowns. Hikers in July often witness these young trees literally springing back up out of their winter tombs beneath the melting snowpack.

Mountain hemlock has many picturesque growth-forms that vary from wind-sheared alpine shrubs and natural "bonsai" trees to graceful or giant trees set in meadows of heather and wildflowers with streams and glistening granite boulders. Thus, mountain hemlock country in the Sierra seems somewhat like a succession of Japanese gardens. The resemblance is not accidental; hemlocks from Oriental mountain forests have long been a favorite of Japanese horticulturists.

However, mountain hemlock differs considerably in appearance from the more common eastern hemlock and western hemlock of North America. The latter have sparser foliage. Their needles are flat and grow mainly from opposite sides of the twigs, while mountain hemlock needles are rounded and plump looking and they clothe the branchlets all

around, including unique little spur shoots which are prevalent. Cones of these other hemlocks are an inch long or less, while those of mountain hemlock average two inches or longer.

The shape and arrangement of the needles and the large-sized cones of mountain hemlock have more in common with spruce (*Picea*) than with hemlocks in general; John Muir referred to this species as the "Hemlock Spruce." In 1949 a French botanist theorized that mountain hemlock was actually a hybrid of spruce and hemlock; but more recently, detailed genetic studies have tended to confirm that mountain hemlock is indeed a true hemlock. A point of confusion about "hemlock" itself is its connection with the fatal potion of hemlock that Socrates drank; "poison hemlock" is an herb in the parsley family.

Mountain hemlock can be found along highways crossing high passes in the Sierra south of Lake Tahoe. Interesting groves occur along the road from Tenaya Lake to Tioga Pass in Yosemite and at Mammoth Mountain ski area. Farther south hemlocks are scattered in moist pockets among the peaks well into Kings Canyon National Park; but the species reaches its southern outpost rather abruptly in a wet site near Silliman Lake in Sequoia National Park. It seems significant that mountain hemlock thus reaches its southern limit in North American within 35 miles of where the West's southern-most glaciers dwell. Both are phenomena of the cloudy and snowy climate engulfing mountains of the North Pacific Coast.

mountain hemlock
Tsuga mertensiana

giant sequoia

Sequoiadendron giganteum
Redwood family (*Taxodiaceae*)

Gigantic tree with cinnamon-colored trunk, inhabiting only a narrow belt within the cool Sierra Nevada forest zone.

Even without giant sequoia, the coniferous forest of the Sierra Nevada would probably rank as one of the most magnificent on earth; but the presence of this species erases all uncertainty. While the most obvious feature setting sequoia apart from other conifers is its gargantuan size, even the fact that it is the world's largest tree cannot account for the fascination it has stirred among humans, prompting so many books to be written about this one rare conifer.

To anyone viewing this Sierra "bigtree" for the first time, though, its size needs explaining first. Why would anyone looking at a bigtree need to have its size explained? Sequoias are so immense that even while looking at them most of us cannot perceive how big they really are.

Old-growth giant sequoias *average* 10 to 15 feet in diameter and about 250 feet in height. The three largest trees (General Sherman, General Grant, and the Boole Tree — all in or near Sequoia and Kings Canyon National Parks) are 27 to 30 feet thick at 4½ feet above the ground. More remarkable is the fact that at a point 120 feet in the air the trunk of General Sherman is still 17 feet in diameter. This tree is 272 feet tall and its first large limb arises so high up on the trunk that it would stretch out over a 12-story office building. This bough is seven feet thick and 125 feet long — much larger itself than record-sized *trees* of many American timber species. A single giant sequoia may contain more wood than is found on a few acres of some of the finest virgin timberland in the Pacific Northwest.

In pioneer days, fallen trunks of giant sequoias served as cabins and stables. A man on horseback rode inside the hollow trunk of a downed sequoia in the Calaveras Grove without having to bend his head. Cut stumps of bigtrees served as dance floors that would accommodate two or three dozen couples.

Quite naturally the discovery of these mammoth conifers in the mid-1800's in what was then a very remote wilderness was greeted with scepticism. When a cross-section from the base of a sequoia 20 feet thick was laborously cut and shipped back East it was promptly dubbed the "California hoax." But loggers lost no time capitalizing on these big trees, which in those days were customarily cut on public lands without regulation or permission from anyone.

The wood of the bigtree — dry weight 18 lb./cubic foot (compared to 32 lb. for Douglas-fir and 53 lb. for Canyon live oak) — is among the lightest of American trees; it is weak and brittle, and its principal desirable quality is a phenomenal resistance to decay. Because of its durability bigtree was sought after for shingles and fenceposts. Between 1862 and the turn of the century Lilliputian lumberjacks struggled with axes and giant crosscut saws for several days to fell a single tree. It took a team of four men 22 days to topple the largest trees.

Slowly, giant after giant thundered to earth and some of the finest stands of sequoias were leveled. The earth trembled and a roar echoed about a mile through the forest when a bigtree crashed to the ground, but when the dust had settled, most of the trunk lay shattered and worthless. Even sound logs were often abandoned as being too big and costly to handle. Finally public sentiment

giant sequoia
Sequoiadendron giganteum

was swayed by John Muir, Newspaperman Colonel George W. Stewart of Visalia, and many others, and the finest remaining groves of bigtrees were included in new national parks and forest reserves to protect them from such destruction.

Many people who have not yet seen the trees find the relationship between California's coast redwood and giant sequoia confusing. Our subject, *Sequoiadendron giganteum*, is known as giant sequoia, "bigtree", or Sierra redwood. It is one of three surviving representatives of an ancient group of conifers whose fossils show that they occupied the landscape from Alaska to the Midwest and Europe to the Orient, including Greenland, during the past few hundreds of millions of years.

Giant sequoia is one of the rarest American trees, being confined to a series of 75 scattered "groves" covering a total of 35,600 acres scattered along a 260-mile stretch of the Sierra mostly between 5000 and 7000 feet elevation. Closely related "coast redwood", *Sequoia sempervirens*, which is the second-largest North American conifer and the world's tallest tree, occupies two million acres of fog belt along the northern California coast and is the source of redwood lumber. Coast redwood has needle-like leaves, while those of giant sequoia are small and scale-like. Until recently giant sequoia was known as *Sequoia gigantea*, but biologists generally agree that differences between redwood and giant sequoia are sufficient to warrant creation of the new genus *Sequoiadendron* for the latter. "Sequoia" is thought to be named in honor of the talented Cherokee Indian who between 1770 and 1843 invented the Cherokee syllabary.

The third sequoia-like tree, which had long been known from fossils, was discovered in 1944 growing in a remote mountainous region of China. This "living fossil" known as the dawn redwood, *Metasequoia*, once grew throughout much of the world, including California. It has foliage somewhat like coast redwood, but is a deciduous conifer.

Giant sequoias inhabit moist sites having similar climates at mid-elevations along the west slope of the Sierra from Placer through Tulare Counties. Annual precipitation here is 45 to 60 inches, most of it coming in November through April as heavy winter snows. Although hardier than coast redwood, giant sequoias are apt to be stunted or killed by severe frost when planted in many of the northern United States. In its snowy Sierra habitat temperatures seldom drop to zero (°F.) and when they do the ground and trees are blanketed deep in snow. Young sequoias are easily distinguished from afar by their dense and narrowly conical crowns; this growth-form makes them popular for ornamental planting.

Sequoiadendron giganteum is an exceptional tree for many reasons besides its giantism. It is not surprising that these huge patriarchs of the forest are among the oldest of living things. The greatest authenticated age of a bigtree is nearly 3200 years derived from counting annual rings on a cut stump. This compares with 2200 years maximum for coastal redwood, but is substantially less than the approximately 5000-year maximum known age for bristlecone pine in eastern Nevada. Detailed studies conducted during the past decade by Dr. Richard Hartesveldt indicate that ages of bigtree have been over-estimated. It now seems probable that the General Sherman tree is less than 2500 years old, General Grant under 2000, and Yosemite National Park's Grizzly Giant is estimated to be 2700 years.

A lesser-known aspect of bigtree, however, is that it grows exceptionally fast throughout its life. Studies suggest that General Grant and

General Sherman may be among the fastest growing trees in the world. They add about 0.04 to 0.06 inch of radial growth to their massive boles each year, which is roughly equivalent to the total volume of wood in a tree 1½ feet thick and 60 feet tall.

So many characteristics of bigtree seem remarkable that perhaps it would be best to start at the beginning, with the seed which is so small that it takes 91,000 of them to make a pound. Usually sequoias do not produce any quantity of cones until they are about two centuries old; but mature trees bear a bountiful crop. Pollen cones ripen in mid to late winter giving the crowns a golden cast while the groves are blanketed in powdery snowpack. The distinctive female or seed-producing cones mature in their second year, when they are about the size and shape of a large chicken egg. However, the mature cone may remain green and carry out photosynthesis like a leaf for 10 years or even longer before its stalk is at last severed, allowing the cone to dry and shed its seed. The cone stalks even produce annual rings like a tree trunk.

Nature speeds up the process of seed planting through its hyperactive furry agent, the chickaree. While this small non-hibernating squirrel eats the larger seeds of pines and firs, he relishes the fleshy scales of sequoia cones and does not bother with the tiny seeds, which are released and scattered about during his feast. Very large sequoias on good sites may bear 40,000 cones, each holding 100 to 300 seeds, and a single chickaree has been known to cut 10,000 cones in a season.

But the chances that any given seed will ultimately produce another giant like its parent approach one in a billion. To start with, a high proportion of seed is not viable. Moreover, in order to germinate, let alone to become a successful

seedling that produces its own food, a seed must land on bare mineral soil rather than thick conifer-needle duff. Appreciable areas of mineral soil in sequoia groves are exposed only occasionally by forest fires.

Natural fire has been suppressed by man for over half a century in the sequoia groves, and biologists have already noted an alarming trend. Dense undergrowth of shade-tolerant white fir and some incense-cedar has developed in the formerly open, park-like stands. This build-up of understory fuels seems to invite a holocaust that might even destroy fire-resistant sequoias and pines should a fire strike and inevitably get out of control. On the other hand, extensive observations, experiments, and other evidence gathered since John Muir's time suggests that natural fires in the pine and bigtree forest of California were seldom highly destructive forces.

Within the last several years a program of letting most lightning fires run their natural course in the higher country of Sequoia and Kings Canyon National Parks has been quite successful. Fire in a controlled form has also been cautiously reintroduced into some of the sequoia groves and pine forests.

That bigtrees are highly resistant to death from fire is illustrated by the fact that virtually all of the large living sequoias have multiple fire-scars on their trunks. The top of General Grant has been set afire twice by lightning strikes in the past 20 years; damage was slight although there was little that could be done to stop the blazes 250 feet up in the air. Some bigtrees continue to grow even though fires have completely hollowed out their insides, so that a person can stand inside the trunk and see the sky above as if looking through a big smokestack.

One reason for this fire resistance is sequoia's layer of fibrous bark, one

Western Slope
of the Sierra

12,000'

10,000'

8,000'

6,000'

4,000'

2,000'

300'

WESTERN
WHITE
PINE

MTN. HEMLOCK

LODGEPOLE
PINE

RED
FIR

JEFFREY
PINE

GIANT
SEQUOIA

WHITE
FIR

DOGWOOD

SUGAR
PINE

WHITE
ALDER

INCENSE
CEDAR

BLACK
OAK

PONDEROSA
PINE

OREGON
ASH

KNOBCONE
PINE

CALIF.
BUCKEYE

DIGGER
PINE

LIVE OAK

BLUE OAK

CALIF.
SYCAMORE

WIL

WHITE OAK

GREAT CENTRAL VA

12,000'

*Eastern Slope
of the
Sierra*

FOX
TAIL
PINE

WHITEBARK
PINE

XTAIL
INE

WHITEBARK
PINE

LIMBER
PINE

LODGEPOLE
PINE

10,000'

MTN.
HEMLOCK

QUAKING
ASPEN

RED
FIR

QUAKING
ASPEN

WESTERN
JUNIPER

WESTERN
JUNIPER

ROCKY
CLIFFS

WHITE
FIR

JEFFREY
PINE

8,000'

STREAMSIDE
TREES

MTN.
MAHOGANY

BITTER
CHERRY

WATER
BIRCH

LIVE OAK

BLACK
OAK

SINGLE-LEAF
PINYON

DESERT
ASH

COTTONWOODS

6,000'

TREES OF
STREAMSIDE
&
NARROW CANYONS

WILLOWS

CALIF.
TORREYA

SINGLE-LEAF PINYON
(ON FEW CANYON WALLS)

DESERT BASINS

4,000'

*"Profile of the
Southern Sierra Nevada
showing a typical distribution
of the tree species."*

CALIF.
LAUREL

VOOD

2,000'

300'

to two feet thick on large trees. Perhaps even more important is the tannic acid present in the bole; this same chemical is used in fire extinguishers. Moreover, tannin pigment secreted into fire scars makes the exposed wood unpalatable to both insects and fungi.

After examining a downed sequoia trunk with a 380-year-old fir growing astride part of it, John Muir concluded that sequoia heartwood does not decay appreciably even after centuries on the damp ground. Visitors to Big Stump Basin (Kings Canyon National Park) and other logged sequoia groves can see piles of sawdust still pink and new-looking even though it has lain there for more than 80 years.

Sequoias could seemingly live forever except that over millen-niums of time fire and windstorms do take their toll. The latter have often toppled trees after heavy spring rains or wet snowfalls when the soil is soggy and crowns are weighted with tons of clinging snow. Bigtrees are particularly vulnerable to being tumultuously overthrown in high winds under these conditions because their root systems lie so shallow, although the feeder roots of a bigtree may spread out into as much as an acre of ground. Several giants met such a fate in 1969, one of them being the famous "tree you can drive through," the Wawona Tree in Yosemite's Mariposa Grove. This 2200-year-old tree crashed to earth because of a heavy load of snow coupled with its lean and the effect of the tunnel cut through the trunk by mankind, which weakened the venerable tree's root-support system.

incense-cedar
Calocedrus decurrens

incense-cedar

Calocedrus decurrens
Cypress family (*Cupressaceae*)

Large tree with lace-like foliage and dense conical crown on middle mountain slopes of California and Oregon.

Many a visitor to the Sierra forest at first mistakes incense-cedars for giant sequoias. During the first century or two of their lives both trees develop symmetrical crowns, making them appear from a distance like perfect triangles. They are both densely clothed in sprays of scaly, lace-like foliage, each has heavily buttressed trunks clad with deeply furrowed orange-brown bark, and veteran incense-cedars, like the sequoias, often show scars of several fires on their trunks.

But, after a visitor has looked at both trees carefully he will see beyond their superficial resem-

blance. Although incense-cedars may grow to be quite large — five or six feet thick and 140 feet tall in moist canyons — they are minia-ture trees by sequoia standards. The triangular form of young incense-cedars is much broader than that of the spire-like sequoias. The beauti-ful bright-green plumes of cedar foliage contrast with darker-green cord-like twigs of giant sequoia. In-cense-cedar boughs are made up of scale-like leaves tightly appressed on the twigs, while pointed sequoia leaves spread from the branchlets like little awls. The bark of old-growth incense-cedar is more of a cinnamon color, whle that of sequoia is rich reddish brown, a dif-ference difficult to describe but easy to see. The plentiful cones of incense-cedar could hardly be con-fused with those of any other tree. When green they are shaped like little urns an inch long; at maturity they become brown, the two scales bending back from the axis of the cone in a manner resembling a duck's bill wide-open with the tongue extended straight out.

Also unlike sequoia, incense-cedar is among the most common trees in the mountains of California and western Oregon. *It is confined to the western slope of the Sierra in our region, and inhabits the lower elevations of the forest, mostly between about 3500 and 6500 feet.*

Until rather recently botanists classified incense-cedar as a member of the diverse genus *Libocedrus,* which was cited as the only genus of conifers encircling the Pacific Ocean — its species growing in mountain forests of California, South America, New Zealand, New Caledonia, New Guinea, southern China, and Taiwan. However, detailed investigations of these trees showed that cones of the three species growing north of the Equator differ markedly in structure from the others. Thus, the California incense-cedar and two Oriental species were reclassified in the new genus, *Calocedrus* ("beautiful cedar"). Like incense-cedar, the other species of *Calocedrus* are important timber trees having rot-resistant wood. Large Chinese *Calocedrus* trees which were buried in past geologic ages have been perfectly preserved and are sometimes "mined" and sawn into coffin stock.

The common name incense-cedar is indeed appropriate for this tree whose heartwood is used for fragrant cedar chests, and whose

leaves give off a pungent aromatic odor when crushed. Other product uses for incense-cedar include shingles, railroad ties, and wood for pencils. Sierra Indians used the durable fibrous bark to make huts called "oochums." This bark, up to six inches thick on old trees, was used by pioneers as roofing for their cabins.

As John Muir describes, the trees themselves also afford a homey shelter: "In its prime, the whole tree is thatched with (beautiful fern-like plumes) . . . so that they shed off rain and snow like a roof, making fine mansions for storm-bound birds and mountaineers." Muir also recounted that, "As it becomes older, . . . Large special branches put out at right angles from the trunk, form big, stubborn elbows, and then shoot up parallel with the axis. Very old trees are usually dead at the top, the main axis protruding above ample masses of green plumes, gray and lichen-covered, and drilled full of acorn holes by the woodpeckers."

Incense-cedar produces pollen in mid-winter, causing hay fever at an unusual time of year, and prompting some human residents of the Sierra to long for a winter storm to settle the pollen dust. Copious pollen and female cone crops of incense-cedar bring about an abundance of curious little seedlings in spring. New cedars just a few inches high exhibit several types of leaves: a pair of inch-long needle-like seed-leaves (cotyledons) at the base; shorter needles giving way to prickly awls farther up the stem; then tiny scale-like leaves at ends of the first year's shoots.

Seedlings of incense-cedar grow slower than those of its common associates, ponderosa and sugar pines. In one study incense-cedar roots grew only 12 inches the first year, while pine roots reached down 20 inches. Unlike the pines, however, incense-cedar can successfully reproduce in conifer-needle litter.

Furthermore, incense-cedar, and also white fir, are tolerant of shade. Consequently, these two species will eventually replace pines and sequoia in the forest unless natural fires (or a substitute such as prescribed fires) are allowed to burn in order to open up the stands and expose mineral soil.

Incense-cedar is hyphenated for the same reason as is Douglas-fir. Incense-cedar is not really a cedar.

In fact, there are no native true cedars (genus *Cedrus*) in North America. The giant western red-cedar of the Pacific Northwest coast and eastern "cedars" are *Thujas* (Arborvitaes) or junipers. The only true cedars — cedar of Lebanon, deodar, and Atlas cedars — are native to the eastern Mediterranean, northern Africa, and the Himalayas, respectively. They have needle-like leaves and do not resemble the trees we call "cedar."

western juniper

Juniperus occidentalis
Cypress family (*Cupressaceae*)

Gnarled, burly little tree of dry rocky sites in the High Sierra and eastern Oregon.

Many writers have described this craggy and weather-beaten, but enduring dweller of the granite cliffs as the most picturesque tree in the High Sierra, quite an accolade considering the competiton. John Muir called the western or Sierra juniper, "a thickset, sturdy, pictur-esque highlander, seemingly content to live for more than a score of centuries on sunshine and snow . . . The burly Juniper, whose girth sometimes more than equals its height, is about as rigid as the rocks on which it grows."

The roots of this hardy tree extend through crevices in the rock, anchoring it to sites where lack of soil, extreme exposure to blizzards, and summer drought do not allow other conifers to survive. Throughout its natural distribution, western juniper commonly grows as an "advance guard" where other trees cannot exist. At its northern limits it occupies hot, arid canyons of the Columbia Basin, a few hundred feet above sea level in sites receiving eight inches average annual precipitation. Western juniper alternates with big sagebrush in dominating eastern Oregon's high desert — juniper colonizing rocky ground but

giving way to sagebrush where there is soil. *In the southern High Sierra, western juniper is at home among the domes, crags, and cliffs on both slopes of the range at 6500 to 10,500 feet.* It is not likely to be confused with other Sierra trees; juniper's distinctive features include minute scale-like leaves on bushy boughs, blue berry-like cones, squatty life-form, and a rocky habitat.

It frequently survives storms and sun for 1000 years, and the bulky bark-stripped and weather-polished trunks and tattered crowns look their age. A western juniper growing several miles from Sonora Pass is apparently the grandfather of all the world's dozens of juniper species. That is, this Methuselah, known as the Bennett Juniper, is the largest-known juniper (13½ feet thick and 87 feet tall) and has been conservatively estimated to be 3000 years old.

Ancient junipers, growing in their characteristic "rocky steadfastness", can be seen along trails in upper canyons throughout much of the Sierra, except along the east slope of the range south of Mammoth Lakes, where they are scarce. They can be found growing on austere granite sites near roads at Tenaya Lake and Mineral King as well as on Sonora Pass and other high summits of the range.

The erratic distribution of western juniper in the Sierra, with individual trees sometimes a mile or more from the nearest seed source, emphasizes the role of birds and other animals in disseminating juniper seed. Experiments have shown that much juniper seed will not germinate unless it has passed through the alimentary tract of some bird or mammal. The rich bluish berry-like fruits mature in fall and cling to the trees all winter; thus they form an excellent food supply for mountain birds. Dr. E.A. Mearns found that 900 berries of Rocky Mountain juniper passed through a Bohemian waxwing in

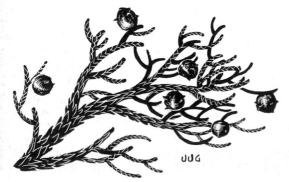

JJG

47

western juniper
Juniperus occidentalis

five hours. Another scientist estimated that bird dissemination of juniper seed makes up two-thirds of the total seeding in natural stands. Humans also have made use of juniper "berries" as the flavoring for gin. Since many junipers bear male and female cones on separate trees, some trees never produce berries.

In high rangeland of northeastern California and Oregon, juniper foliage is sometimes consumed eagerly by deer and livestock. Usually the herbivores are not very fond of this scaly-leaved tree, but, for some undiscovered reason, on certain trees they will devour all branches within reach — the deer standing up on their hind legs.

As anyone who has seen the exposed wood in "living snags" of juniper might suspect, heartwood of this species is exceedingly durable. It has been used for fence posts on the western range. The wood is also heavy, tough, reddish in color, and pleasantly aromatic. California Indians are said to have used the pitch to fasten feathers to arrow shafts, and, by rubbing the pitch into these shafts, they made their arrows more durable.

A mystifying juniper grows near the High Sierra Trail below Hamilton Lake in Sequoia National Park. This tree has a 200-pound granite boulder wedged in a fork 15 feet above the ground. Although this juniper grows in an opening away from nearby granite domes, one geologist was able to supply a plausible explanation: The stone was swept down in a spring avalanche when the snowpack was 10 or more feet thick; it landed in a pile of snow atop the crown, and when the snow melted the boulder settled gently into a crotch of the tree without causing damage.

Spiral grain is a phenomenon found in the growth of most, perhaps all, western conifers, but it is much more pronounced in trees growing under harsh climatic conditions, like Sierra juniper and foxtail pine. Why does the grain of some trees (and sometimes a strip of bark keeping the tree alive) corkscrew up into the air like a barber's pole? One hypothesis is that enzymes causing growth in the tree's cambium or sap layer are influenced by the spinning of the earth — like water draining out of a sink, which is said to twist one way in the Northern Hemisphere and the opposite way south of the Equator. Unfortunately this fails to explain why trees in the same stand sometimes spiral in different directions although the Equator certainly does not run between them!

OTHER JUNIPERS

Three other junipers, although rare, are present in the Sierra. Utah juniper [*Juniperus osteosperma*] is a tall shrub (10-15 ft.) of the Great Basin desert that reaches the lower skirts of the Sierra east of Yosemite. It can be found near Hot Creek Geysers east of Mammoth Lakes. California juniper [*Juniperus californica*] is a shrub (4-12 ft. tall) of the coastal range foothills that reportedly extends inland to the lowermost slopes of the Sierra, about 25 miles west of Yosemite National Park. Both these shrubby junipers are distinguished from tree-like western juniper by their reddish berries that have a sweet, dry pulp. Western juniper berries are dark blue at maturity and have a resinous pulp.

Common juniper (*Juniperus communis*) forms a mat-like shrub usually under two feet high in western North America, although in the Northeast and in Northern Europe it sometimes develops into a small tree. It has small curved needle-like leaves and is the only conifer species that grows all around the northern end of the globe, from Alaska to Greenland to Eurasia. Common juniper has been reported to grow at high elevations from Mono Pass northward in the Sierra.

California torreya

Torreya californica
Yew family (*Taxaceae*)

Small spiny-leaved evergreen growing in ravines and rocky gorges at lower elevations in the California mountains.

California torreya is a curious little tree which, like the great sequoia, has an ancient lineage but today occupies a very restricted range. Torreya is commonly known as "California-nutmeg," because its plum-like fruit resembles that of nutmeg, the spice. However, similarity between torreya and nutmeg is superficial — the latter is a broadleaved tree of the tropics, while torreya is a member of the yew family, and thus a conifer.

The name *Torreya* honors the outstanding American botanist John Torrey (1796-1873), who first discovered this group of trees when he found the Florida torreya — even rarer than its California kin — in the 1830's. In addition to the two North American torreyas, three species survive in parts of China and Japan. These are mere remnants of a much greater distribution in the geologic past; fossils show that their ancestors grew in the Arctic as well as across North American and Europe.

Finding California torreya requires considerable knowledge of where to search and what to look for. The species reaches its best development on cool shady slopes and in canyons of the coastal mountains in Lake and Mendocino Counties; it inhabits the draws and basins on Mount Tamalpais in Marin County. Also, *it grows in various rocky gorges and ravines scattered along most of the western slope of the Sierra Nevada between 2000 and 6000 feet elevation. Torreyas line the road entering El Portal. Other good places to find them include Hetch Hetchy, the entrance to Boyden Cave in Kings Canyon, and the trail to Crystal Cave and near Clough Cave in Sequoia National Park.*

At first glance it may look like an especially deep-green Douglas-fir poking its young crown out above the canyon live oaks and chaparral. However, in the south-central Sierra, torreya typically occupies rocky gulches too low and hot for Douglas-fir or areas beyond Douglas-fir's southern range limits. Inspection of the foliage reveals long (1½ - 2 inches), broad, lance-like needles, glossy green on top and as sharp as cactus spines. These leaves will not be confused with those from other Sierra trees. When the foliage or stem of a torreya is bruised it gives off a pungent aromatic or foul odor, which is the origin for torreya's other common name, "stinking cedar."

The fruit, which botanists classify as an "aril" is a modified cone, blue-green, plum-like, and 1 - 1¾ inches long. The big (125/lb.), rich seeds

California torreya
Torreya californica

were harvested and roasted by Indians for eating. The fruits hang from tips of outer branches on *female* trees in late summer and autumn. In contrast to most other Sierra conifers, which produce both male (pollen) and female (cone) flowers on the same tree, each torreya bears flowers of only one sex. Some large torreyas never yield fruit, simply because they are male trees.

In the Sierra canyons, torreyas rarely attain two feet in diameter and 60 feet in height. Small size, coupled with their dense crowns gives them a youthful appearance; nevertheless trees only 1 - 1½ feet thick are likely to be two centuries old. Torreya and coast redwood are notable among the world's conifers in their ability to sprout permanent new trunks from cut or burned stumps. In this respect torreya, like the chaparral shrubs, is adapted to foothill fires.

Wood of torreya is strong, elastic, and durable, and is said to have been used by certain California Indians to make hunting bows. In these characteristics it is similar to wood of its relative, the yew tree (*Taxus*), which furnished stock for the archers of medieval Europe. One species of yew, *Taxus brevifolia*, is native to the Pacific Northwest, where it often grows as a small tree. Pacific yew extends southward in shrubby form along the western slope of the Sierra, where it was previously reported as far south as Tulare County. Recent investigations, however, suggest that its southern outpost is really Calaveras County (North Grove, Calaveras Big Trees State Park).

tree willow
Salix

tree willows

Salix spp.
Willow family (*Salicaceae*)

Willow (*Salix*) is one of the most cosmopolitan genera of trees and shrubs. Several hundred species and varieties of willow occupy the landscape from southern South America and Africa to the Arctic. About 175 species are native to North America; but only 30 of them attain tree size and even these are usually small trees. Five of the approximately two dozen Sierra willows are generally classified as being tree-like, and are described briefly here; other willows sometimes attain heights of 10-20 feet. The enthusiastic reader is referred to Munz's CALIFORNIA FLORA for a complete listing.

While it is easy to distinguish a willow from other trees and shrubs, identifying individual species of willow can be quite a challenge even for a trained botanist. In some cases positive identification may require examination of both male

and female flowers (catkins), which are, however, borne on different plants! Willows are deciduous and have long and narrow, simple (not compound or divided) leaves which are attached in an alternate arrangement to the slender, often yellow or reddish twigs. Twigs of various willows were once widely used by Sierra Indians for making baskets.

Willow flowers arranged in long, narrow clusters called catkins or "pussy willows" bloom before the leaves appear in spring, often while snow still blankets the ground. The female catkins have long been prized for bouquets; their appearance in February or March brings the promise of spring to winter-weary inhabitants of the mountains. Male catkins are often collected by mistake since they generally have a similar fuzzy or felt-like texture. Closer inspection, however, reveals yellow stamens projecting from the male catkins, and they are to be avoided for bouquets because they soon shed stamens and pollen about the house.

As spring progresses the minute

52

individual flowers which make up the female catkin mature into capsules containing seeds so tiny that it takes two or three million to make a pound. Each seed has a tuft of hair which allows it to be buoyed over long distances by a canyon breeze. Moreover, because the willow is so often found lining a mountain stream or river, the seeds are often transported by water. Considering how tiny these seeds are it is not surprising that they have little stored food or protective covering. Unlike the much heavier kernels of pines or oaks, willow seeds do not remain dormant over the winter, but instead germinate within about 24 hours of being shed.

Willows are generally intolerant of shade and dry soils, and the chances of successful germination and survival of this frail seed are extremely poor. Nature compensates for these adverse odds by producing such prodigious numbers of seeds that some do by chance happen to find a vacant niche on a moist sandy river bar or the like and, under just the right conditions of temperature, the species may reproduce. Furthermore, even without seed production willow could flourish, since new trees sprout readily from roots and stumps. The trees themselves are composed of light, weak wood, and a single trunk seldom survives 50 winters.

Willows can easily be distinguished from other Sierra trees even in winter by the fact that their buds are covered with but a single scale rather than several overlapping scales. Willows inhabit moist sites from the tropics to the Arctic, and in California they grow from tidewater and from springs in the deserts up to well above timberline in the Sierra. Two species of dwarf alpine willows cover perpetually-moist, snowy slopes as high as 12,000 feet in elevation. Branching systems of these tiny shrubs are buried beneath the surface and their growth form is like a well-trimmed lawn, but in this case complete with catkins that thrust up two inches from the glacial ground in August.

Valley willow [Salix gooddingii] derives its common name from California's Great Central Valley where it grows along the rivers, extending as high up as 2000 feet into the western foothills of the Sierra Nevada. A variety of this species also inhabits the lower east slope of the Sierra. Valley willow is commonly a spreading tree forked from the base and 20 to 45 feet tall. It can be told from all other southwestern willows in that its yellowish twigs snap off neatly and easily when pulled, rather than tearing. This characteristic is probably one reason why valley willow is so widespread along watercourses in the desert southwest. The broken twigs readily root in wet sand and develop into a new tree. Desert travelers have regarded valley willow as a special friend for it is a sure sign of water. Some southwestern Indians used split twigs of this willow for weaving water-tight baskets.

Red or smooth willow. [Salix laevigata] is widespread along rushing mountain streams in the Sierra foothills below about 5000 feet elevation. It attains a height of 15 to 40 feet and derives its two common names from its smooth, shining

JJG   *Salix lasiandra*

foliage and twigs that are often reddish.

Pacific willow [Salix lasiandra] grows along rivers in the Great Central Valley and lines snow-fed streams up to 8000 feet in the Sierra. It can be identified by glandular-warty leaf stalks (look for two or more black spots on the leaf stem at its juncture with the blade), and by its long, narrow, dark-green leaves. Spanish Californians made their saddletrees from this willow, which forms trees 20 to 50 feet tall. Especially large Pacific Willows can be found along the lower Sacramento River. This species and other willows and alders form dense thickets in the wetlands all but impenetrable to man. Such protected stands along watercourses are a Mecca for wildlife, providing ideal nesting sites for dozens of bird species as well as habitat for deer, mink, garter snakes, trogs, etc., and shady pools for trout.

Arroyo or white willow (*Salix lasiolepis*) forms a small tree (6-30 feet) that can be distinguished by smooth light-colored bark on younger trunks and limbs, which is often blotched with nearly white areas. *It occupies streamsides from the Central Valley up to about 7000 feet in the Sierra and is also found in the narrow canyons of desert mountains. It can be seen locally at Hospital Rock on the Middle Fork of the Kaweah River in Sequoia National Park and at Mineral King.*

Scouler or mountain willow (*Salix scouleriana*) differs from other tree willows in being able to colonize mountain slopes away from water courses. It forms an arborescent shrub (5-30 feet tall) with many slender, erect stems arising from a clump. *It grows high up in the mountains, to 10,000 feet,* and has been called fire willow because throughout much of its vast range from the Rockies to Alaska it readily sprouts or seeds over large areas which have been swept by forest fires.

Scouler or mountain willow

black cottonwood

Populus trichocarpa
Willow family (*Salicaceae*)

Black cottonwood is the largest American poplar and the tallest broadleaf tree in the West. In the rich bottomlands of the Pacific Northwest black cottonwoods loft their spreading crowns as high as 175 feet into the damp air. Such trees may live for more than two centuries and they are supported by massive, clear boles, often four to six feet in diameter and covered with thick, heavily-furrowed gray bark. Along Sierra streams black cottonwoods commonly attain diameters of two or three feet and heights of 80 feet.

Although this species thrives in wet valleys along the North Pacific Coast (as far north as Anchorage, Alaska) where annual rainfall often exceeds 100 inches, it also extends into deserts of southern California and Nevada where yearly precipitation is less than 10 inches. In dry regions including the Sierra Nevada, however, black cottonwood grows where its roots can capture the water from streams, springs, lakes, marshes, or wet meadows.

The fact that cottonwoods use and store large quantities of water is frequently illustrated to foresters who attempt to age such trees using an increment borer; when this hollow drill penetrates the trunk of a big cottonwood, a stream of water is apt to gush out.

Black cottonwood can be distinguished from other Sierra trees by its large, broad, almost triangular, pointed leaves. Also, it bears great pointed buds covered with several shiny scales. The buds are filled with a sticky, resinous substance that looks and feels somewhat like strawberry jam. This resin gives off a strong balsam odor — like that of New England's balsam poplar. But, this western balsam poplar is an even grander resident of the wetlands than its eastern kin. Its massive boughs provide splendid nesting platforms for ospreys, bald eagles, blue herons, and Canada geese, while cavities in the rotting trunks are used by woodpeckers, great horned owls and even wood ducks.

Cottonwood grows rapidly (one Northwestern tree 120 feet tall and 32 inches thick was only 27 years old!) and produces weak, light, clear wood used for boxes and barrels. Stumps sprout readily, and fresh-cut twigs will grow into new trees if planted into wet ground. In fact Lombardy poplar, which because of its distinctive upswept limbs has been used throughout much of the Northern Hemisphere as an ornamental and windbreak tree, has been propagated entirely from cuttings that originally came from a tree in Italy. This tree did not reproduce its kind through seeds. Black cottonwood logs left through the rainy winter and spring on railroad cars in western Washington soon produced a small grove of vigorous sprouts.

Cottonwoods, like willows, bear male and female flowers on separate trees. The female flowers mature into four-inch-long hanging clusters of fruit profusely covered with soft, cottony hairs. The fruiting capsules split open in summer, releasing minute plume-laden seeds into the breezes. When ripened, the downy fruits drift through the air day after day and gradually form piles a few inches deep in sheltered spots on the forest floor. At this season even the casual observer will know why these trees are called "cottonwoods."

Black cottonwood grows all along rivers and even small tributary streams from the western foothills well up into the heart of the Sierra Nevada. It has been reported as high up as 9300 feet, but is normally

black cottonwood
Populus trichocarpa

abundant and well-developed only in the middle and lower canyons, below 6000 feet. It also inhabits the major canyons in the Sierra's east escarpment, where it is associated with thickets of water birch.

On the broad desert slopes beneath the east-side canyons — and beneath the western foothills, also — black cottonwood gives way to another big, spreading poplar known as Fremont cottonwood (*Populus fremontii*). The two species can be distinguished using these criteria: Black cottonwood has leaf stems (petioles) that are round in cross-section (easily tested by rolling the petioles between one's fingers); its leaves are dark green above and rusty or silvery beneath. Fremont cottonwood has leaf stems that are flattened in cross-section, and its leaves are a similar yellowish-green on both surfaces.

While black cottonwood is basically a native of the moist Pacific Northwest, reaching its southern and dry limits in California, Fremont cottonwood is a Southwesterner. It borders rivers and springs beneath the burning desert sun from west Texas to southern California. It was named for John C. Fremont who discovered the large arid-land cottonwoods on his 1844 expedition to Nevada and California. Fremont called them "sweet cottonwoods" because, unlike many other poplars which have bitter bark, the inner bark of this tree was relished by his horses.

Fremont cottonwood is widely distributed in the lowlands west, east, and south of the Sierra and extends into the lower reaches of the east-side canyons south of Lone Pine. It is reported as high up as 6500 feet in the Sierra.

With some botanical sleuthing, two other cottonwoods can be found on the southern Sierra's desert slope. Both lanceleaf cottonwood (*Populus acuminata*) and narrowleaf cottonwood (*Populus angustifolia*) can be distinguished from the others by their relatively narrow leaves — the former having leaves mostly 1½-2 times longer than broad and the latter with leaves 2-5 times. It was thought that lanceleaf cottonwood is a hybrid between narrowleaf cottonwood and one of the broadleaved species, such as Fremont cottonwood. However, in the Sierra and elsewhere lanceleaf cottonwood occurs in the absence of one or another of the suggested parent species. This indicates that although it may have originally developed as a hybrid (tetraploid), this distinct type of cottonwood is probably capable of reproducing through seed. *This tree commonly lines the east-slope streams especially between the lower elevational limits of black cottonwood and the upper limits of Fremont cottonwood. It also inhabits the upper Kern River. Although narrowleaf cottonwood grows in many parts of western North America, it is known in the Sierra only from Division Creek, near Independence at about 6000 feet.*

quaking aspen

Populus tremuloides
Willow family (*Salicaceae*)

Quaking aspen is literally the most colorful tree in the Sierra high-country. In summer it bears leaves that are bright green on top with a silvery underside. These colors come alternately into view as the roundish leaves flutter and whisper incessantly in the light breeze. Much of the charm of an aspen grove lies in the effect of sunlight glinting on creamy white bark that covers the clear boles of the small trees. Scars from old branches make a pattern of dark spots on the gleaming trunks. Also, names and dates etched in aspen bark by sheepherders and wranglers around the turn of the century can still be found occasionally in High Sierra meadows; claw marks where bears have apparently done their honing on aspen trunks also become indelible. Indian summer's brisk, sunny weather brings out an unforgettable display of brilliant yellow, gold, orange, and sometimes even red hues in quaking aspen, shortly before winter descends upon the mountains.

Autumn is an especially good time to observe aspen's "clonal behavior." Although a small grove of aspens is likely to produce millions of tiny seeds (2,000,000/lb.) each year, few of them are viable and new aspens produced from seeds are considered a rarity in much of the Mountain West. Instead, aspen reproduces through sprouts. New shoots arise from stumps of existing root systems, especially after fire. Also, the groves called "clones" because each tree arises from a common root system, expand by root-sprouting seedlings to fill the available habitat.

That trees in a clone are genetically identical and yet distinct from those in other clones is apparent to someone visiting the high-country in early autumn. Some aspen groves will be golden, others yellowish, and others still green; thus the clones enter winter dormancy at different times. Biologists have discovered that the date when aspen and many other trees turn color is not necessarily related to the first hard frost as was formerly believed. Detailed greenhouse experiments varying the length of daylight have shown that many species of trees from sites in different latitudes leaf out, flower, and drop their leaves each season in a genetically-controlled response to a certain length of daylight ("photoperiod"), or even to the duration of darkness. This photoperiodic response is also a force that triggers animal behavior, as for instance the "biological clock" that causes the swallows to return to Capistrano. The activity of each aspen clone may be in response to a somewhat different photoperiod.

Quaking aspen can be told from cottonwoods and other Sierra trees by several characteristics. Smooth, light bark on mature aspens contrasts with the rough bark on cottonwoods and most other species; aspen's small buds are shiny but not filled with resin like the much larger cottonwood buds. But perhaps most diagnostic are aspen leaves. The leaf blades are almost round except for their pointed tip, and they average 1-1½ inches across. Because they are borne on long stalks (petioles) which are flattened or "lopsided" in cross-section, the leaves quiver in the slightest breeze. Early French-Canadian trappers reportedly believed that this tree furnished wood for the Cross and since then has never ceased trembling.

Quaking aspen has one of the widest distributions of any tree in North America, and a similar species (*Populus tremula*) inhabits Eurasia. Quaking aspen occupies our continent from the edge of the Arctic tundra from Alaska to Labrador southward to Virginia and at increasing elevations in the western mountains well into Mexico. *Aspen grows throughout the southern Sierra between 6000 and 10,000 feet in moist meadows or in rock-piles, especially at the bases of cliffs where there is ample ground water.*

Being very intolerant of shade and competition from conifers, aspen does not inhabit the dense forest. Its buds, bark and shoots are a favorite food of wildlife including beaver and deer; domestic stock readily eat it also. Aspens usually live only 50-60 years, attaining about a foot in diameter and 50-60 feet in height.

Aspen country was the favorite haunt of early trappers in the Great Central Valley and throughout much of the mountain West because aspen meant beaver. An aspen stick placed strategically in a hole in a beaver's dam was the bait that lured millions of flat-tails to death in the steel-jawed trap so that men in Eastern cities could sport beaver hats. By the mid-1800's beaver was nearly exterminated; then fortunately fashion changed and beaver, no longer in vogue, was permitted to survive.

quaking aspen
Populus tremuloides

white alder

Alnus rhombifolia
Birch family (*Betulaceae*)

About 30 species of alder trees and shrubs inhabit stream bottoms, swampy ground, and high mountains throughout much of the Northern Hemisphere, and extend southward in the Andes as far as Peru. Like other members of the birch family, alders bear both male and female flowers on the same tree. These flowers grow in hanging clusters or aments, somewhat like those of cottonwood; however the alder's female fruit is a distinctive little woody catkin that looks like the cone of a conifer. In winter Sierra alders can be distinguished

by their prominent brown buds which stand out on a short stalk and have a coating of light fuzz.

White alders 50-70 feet tall and a foot or more in diameter grow in dense thickets along streams from the Great Central Valley up to about 5000 feet on the western slope of the Sierra. They grow abundantly at Happy Isles, Mirror Lake, and in places along the banks of the Merced River in Yosemite, and are common along most foothill streams in Sequoia National Park and vicinity.

Woodsmen often consider white alder a more reliable indicator of running water than the cottonwood, willow, or even sycamore with which they are frequently associated, since alder is usually confined to streams that run all summer. The bark of young alders contrasts with that of other streamside trees in being smooth and steel-gray and having distinctive upsidedown-V-shaped marks where the branches start. Unlike neighboring cottonwoods, aspen, willows, and maples, white alder does not turn color in autumn, but drops its 2-to-4-inch-long leaves while they are still essentially green.

The little cone-like catkins dangle in alder trees all year, however, to the apparent delight of pine siskins and flocks of grosbeaks and purple finches which attack the fruits and gobble up tiny seeds during winter and spring.

Mountain alder (*Alnus tenuifolia*) usually grows as a tall shrub in swampy sites between 4500 and 8300 feet elevation on the western slope of the southern Sierra. In mucky swales on the mountainsides its stems bend almost to a horizontal position, making such patches of "slide alder" almost impenetrable. The margins of mountain alder leaves have fine teeth superimposed upon rather coarse sawteeth, while leaves of white alder have only the fine serrations.

white alder
Alnus rhombifolia

JJ GYER

water birch

Betula occidentalis
Birch family (*Betulaceae*)

In summer, when an overheated traveler mounts the dry eastern slope of the Sierra Nevada above the burning sagebrush plains, he will see lines of lovely little birch trees reminiscent of cooler climates. They extend down along the stream-courses toward him, like streamers flowing out from the cool mountain forests. About 40 species of birch trees and shrubs occupy the Northern Hemisphere. Birch is a major forest tree throughout the north-eastern United States, Canada, Alaska, Siberia, and northern Europe, and low shrubby forms of birch colonize vast areas of the Arctic tundra. However, only one species, water birch, inhabits the Sierra.

This tree's technical name means "western birch," and in fact it does grow on mountain streams throughout much of the inland West from nothern Arizona and New Mexico to southern British Columbia and Manitoba. "Water birch" is aptly named since it is found almost exclusively bordering streams or ponds; sometimes it even grows squeezed into a slit-like rock gorge where water gushes over its roots.

In the Sierra water birch is reported from scattered locations between 2000 and 8000 feet on the western slope — including Kings Canyon, Charlotte Creek, and Junction Meadow in Kings Canyon National Park. However, it more commonly borders streams draining into the Owens Valley on the eastern slope between about 5000 and 9000 feet. Groves of multi-stemmed, slender birch averaging perhaps 20 feet tall shade the creeks and ponds at Whitney Portal and near Glacier Lodge on Big Pine Creek. This shading helps to produce better habitat for trout which lurk in eddies among the birch roots. It may seem surprising that this water-dependent tree occupies ravines and springs in high desert ranges near Death Valley. Thus, it clings to snow-fed mountain brooks even in regions were these cooling waters are destined to descend into and disappear upon an alkali lake bed.

Like alder, birch bears both sexes of flowers on the same tree. The female catkins of birch, however, are solitary, while those of alder grow in clusters. Also, birch catkins disintegrate when ripe unlike the persistent alder "cones."

Although usually much smaller, water birch sometimes produces trunks nearly a foot thick and 50 feet tall. Its coppery or glossy dark bronze bark, somewhat like that of cherry, does not peel like other birch bark, and its slender young twigs can be readily identified by their rough, warty texture, because they are covered with resinous glands. Water birch's deep green form beneath the searing summer sun, and its bright yellow foliage in the crisp autumn air highlight many a stream threading its way through the stark sagebrush prairies of the American West.

water birch
Betula occidentalis

California white oak

Valley Oak

Quercus lobata
Beech family (*Fagaceae*)

Perhaps 500 species of oak trees and shrubs occupy the northern half of the globe; about 60 species of tree-like oaks grow as natives in the United States. The western states generally have comparatively few oaks; California with its ten tree oaks and six shrubby species is an exception.

California white oak, more commonly known as valley oak, is the monarch among deciduous oaks in the West. In fact, its massive form compares with that of the great eastern white oak (*Quercus alba*) and famous English oak (*Quercus robur*). When Captain George Vancouver explored the Santa Clara Valley in 1796 he thought it had been planted with English oaks!

Quercus lobata is so named for its deeply lobed leaves. It can be distinguished from other California oaks by the light-colored, deeply fissured or "checkered" bark; its oak-like leaves that are green and lobed; and its shallow, knobby acorn cup which holds the long, pointed nut. A number of common names have been applied to this species which further reflect upon its characteristics.

One of the most historical epithets was "roble", used by early Europeans in California who found its magnificent groves reminiscent of the stately *Quercus robur* of their native land. "Valley oak" was aptly applied by early settlers who noted this tree's affinity for gentle valley habitats, and soon recognized it as an indicator of fertile loamy soil. The reference "water oak" may have applied to the relatively shallow water table usually found beneath these oaks; ground water thus tapped by the great tree's roots enable them to survive California's often severe, four-month-long summer drought. "Weeping oak" was used in reference to the distinctive, slender branchlets that dangle earthward from the broad crowns.

"California white oak" is the name accepted by the U. S. Forest Service. It associates this species with other white oaks as opposed to red or black oaks. The latters' acorns mature in their second year, usually have a fine felt-like coating on the inner side of the shell, and bear bitter seed. White oak acorns mature in one season, have no inner felt, and bear sweet seed. Furthermore, leaves of white oaks have smooth lobes while lobes of the others are bristle- or spiny-tipped. *Quercus lobata* grows only in California valleys, normally back at least a few miles from the sea. *It occurs west of the Sierra Nevada from the vicinity of Redding southward to the San Fernando Valley between sea level and as high as 4000 feet elevation in valleys of the southern Sierra.*

One of the finest remaining stands

California white oak
Quercus lobata

of valley oak can be seen in the Kaweah River drainage immediately south of Visalia. Also, by traveling eastward up the Kaweah toward the entrance to Sequoia National Park a visitor can see an array of valley oaks along with blue and canyon live oaks scattered across the green or golden grasslands. The community of Big Oak Flat on the northern entrance road to Yosemite was named by Forty-niners for a giant white oak said to be eleven feet thick that was rooted in the "flat" or mountain valley. Four miles farther up this winding mountain road at the ghost town of Second Garotte seven men were hanged from another famous white oak for stealing gold from the sluice boxes.

Still another label has been attached to this tree. Some of the early settlers scornfully called it "mush oak" because in sharp

contrast to eastern white oak its wood proved nearly worthless. Hard but brittle, heavy but weak, and prone to rapid decay, it had value only as firewood. For that purpose large trees are said to have yielded 50-90 cords (a cord being a woodpile four feet by four feet by eight feet).

Formerly, California Indians harvested large quantities of valley oak's sweet kernels. The copious mast still provides nourishment for flocks of band-tailed pigeons as well as gray squirrels and Acorn woodpeckers; however, much of it is also fed to hogs. Perhaps the chief value of valley oaks today is their aesthetic appeal and the ample shade they cast, which is welcomed by man or beast beneath the blistering summer sun.

In spite of heavy acorn crops borne

every other year, reproduction of valley oak is poor. Germination requires that the nuts remain covered with fresh soil or litter; agriculture, livestock, and housing developments have taken over much of the rich valley oak habitat, and old, picturesque trees left standing are frequently not being replaced by another generation.

A shrubby form of the Oregon white oak called *Quercus garrayana* var. *semota* can be found on dry sites at 2500 to 5600 feet along the western slope of the southern Sierra. It can be seen along the trail to Crystal Cave in Sequoia National Park.

blue oak

Quercus douglasii
Beech family (*Fagaceae*)

Although they are situated far apart in the botanical "family tree" or classification of plant families, blue oak and Digger pine have very similar geographic ranges. They are confined to almost exactly the same region — arid foothills of northern and central California, south to the Tehachapis and inland to the foot of the Sierra. Both species form spreading trees of modest proportions compared to other oaks or pines, and together they inhabit the driest slopes. On a torrid afternoon in summer a view of this oak's dense bluish form standing out amidst the smoky haze somehow seems to climax the traveler's feeling of oppressive heat.

Blue oak prospers on the parched hillsides, and does not even put out its full complement of foliage until summer has set in. Trees that characteristically occupy arid habitats are frequently capable of faster growth on moist sites, but are kept out of these favorable sites by their inability to successfully compete for "growing room." Blue oak's other common associate, interior live oak, profits from additional water. In contrast, however, irrigation ditches cut too near blue oaks will gradually kill them.

Blue oak occupies the southern Sierra's western skirts, where it grows abundantly between 500 and 2500 feet elevation. It commonly attains 40 to 60 feet in height and about two feet in diameter during its two or three centuries of life. Blue oak can be distinguished from other oaks by its oblong leaves that have only shallow lobes and are deep bluish-green on the upper surface. Like the white oaks, with which it is often grouped, its seed is sweet and the inner surface of its acorn shell is hairless. The bark is light gray and scaly, and although

its twigs are stout they snap off readily.

The wood is close-grained, heavy (55½ lb./cubic ft.), and hard. Sometimes the heartwood is so dense that it will turn an axe; hence settlers called it "iron oak." However, blue oak wood is brittle, susceptible to fungi, and frequently is cross-grained. Old branches usually litter the ground beneath the trees. Although the wood gives off generous warmth when burned, it was selected and used with caution by some pioneer Californians because of the masses of fine mycelial threads, from fungi, that it sometimes contains. These floated up the chimney and alit on the roof while still aglow.

Blue oaks are perhaps most memorable in late April and early May, after the rainy season. This is flowering time both for the oak and the luxuriant blanket of grasses and annual wildflowers that covers the rolling hillsides along with these open-growing trees.

blue oak
Quercus douglasii

California black oak

Quercus kelloggii
Beech family (*Fagaceae*)

California black oak is the largest mountain oak in the West. Indeed, it is almost unmistakable for a variety of reasons. Its sturdy, forked trunk and massive limbs are clad in blackish bark that gives the tree its name. *The trees grow well up in the Sierra canyons and slopes in sandy meadows and pockets of soil among the rockpiles. They inhabit the yellow pine forest belt from about 3500 to 7500 feet elevation on the west slope of the south-central Sierra, and occur slightly higher up on the Sierra's east escarpment.* Black oaks average about three feet thick at maturity and 60-80 feet tall, but gnarled veterans five or more feet through are scattered about the mountainsides, and one tree 36 feet in girth has been reported in Yosemite.

Black oak's leaves set it apart from other oaks of the Sierra in being large (4-10 inches long including the petiole), thin, bright green above, and distinctly lobed with each lobe having bristle tips. Black oak foliage adds colorful charm to the pine forest zone. When the tiny new leaves emerge from their buds, usually in May, they are red and velvety; by June they turn into bright yellow-green foliage that is translucent in the sunshine. In autumn the leaves range from tawny yellow to a rich golden brown.

Black oak occupies the mountain slopes from west-central Oregon south through the Coast Ranges and Sierra to San Diego County. It grows in canyons along the Sierra's desert slope as far south as Shepard Creek near Independence. Sometimes it seems as if this tree actually has an appetite for rocks; trunks that have grown up next to a boulder occasionally produce a callus growth covering the rock as if the tree were in the process of swallowing it!

Although craggy black oaks can be found throughout the Sierra's yellow pine belt, most famous are the stout, spreading oaks surrounding the meadows in the heart of Yosemite Valley. Other fine groves mixed with yellow pine and incense-cedar occupy the sandy glacial valley in the depths of the Kings River Canyon. Although various types of parasitic mistletoe plants infect most species of trees in the Sierra large bushy clusters of mistletoe are especially noticeable in these large oaks in winter and early spring before the trees leaf out.

It is no coincidence that California Indians chose sites like Yosemite and Kings Canyon for their summer encampments. To them black oak groves were akin to our wheatfields. An Indian family ate perhaps 500 pounds of acorns each year. Tribes that summered in the Sierra Nevada harvested great quantities of black oak acorns and pounded them into meal in the mortars (cup-shaped depressions) they had worn into granite bedrock. These native Californians leached the bitter tannic acid out of the acorn meal by pouring or by diverting stream water over it. Although some of the meal was then apparently baked into bread, most of it was cooked and consumed in the family "mush pot" — a water-tight basket. The mush was cooked by placing hot stones from the fire into the basket.

California black oak
Quercus kelloggii

After many centuries or, more likely, millenniums of relying on acorns of the various oaks as their chief daily food the human residents of California no longer consume this nutritious fruit. However, other native Sierrans still attain much of their sustenance from black oak. Deer browse its leaves and sprouts; band-tailed pigeons flock in the trees and eat the mast; western gray squirrels scold raucously at anyone who approaches their private orchards.

The red-topped acorn woodpecker outwits the squirrels in order to glean his share of the crop. This noisy fellow, called *el carpintero* by Spanish Californians, hammers acorn-size holes into poles or tree trunks, then jams the nuts into these pockets, pointed end first, so they are flush with the surface and unobtainable to squirrels. He often stashes away hundreds of acorns in the bark of a single tree. One might think that the sight of such a securely unavailable acorn cache in their own trees would be particularly galling to the feisty squirrels!

Despite the animals' pilfering, many acorns fall into the leaf litter and some of these germinate in the following spring. Survival is precarious in many groves because black oak is even more intolerant of shade than ponderosa pine. Consequently, without natural or prescribed fire, logging, or other disturbance to open up the forest, conifers tend to crowd out the oaks. In many areas the successional sequence is black oak giving way to ponderosa and that in turn to incense-cedar or white fir.

canyon live oak
Quercus chrysolepis

interior live oak
Quercus wislizenii

live oaks

Quercus spp.
Beech family (*Fagaceae*)

Two species of evergreen oak trees, or "live oaks," grow in the Sierra Nevada, and an evergreen hybrid of one of these species with California black oak is also present. *Interior live oak [Quercus wislizenii] forms a short dense tree, whose crown is often twice as broad as tall, growing with the blue oaks and Digger pines of the driest foothill slopes. Canyon live oak [Quercus chrysolepis] forms a medium-sized, spreading tree among the shady gorges, cliffs, and canyon rockpiles, mostly between 3000 and 6000 feet on the west slope of the southern Sierra. It also develops into a shrubby form on drier, more exposed slopes or ridges up to about 8000 feet.*

Both canyon and interior live oaks bear dark green, leathery leaves 1-2½ inches long. The appearance of the leaves is variable; even on the same branch some leaves are apt to have smooth margins, while others have spiny-toothed edges like holly. (Holly, *Ilex*, does not grow naturally in California.)

The fruit probably provides the most reliable characteristics for distinguishing between interior and canyon live oaks. Acorns of the former tend to be slender, usually not more than half an inch wide; those of the latter are ¾ to 1 inch across. Cups of canyon live oak acorns are clothed in yellow fuzz, hence the derivation of the name "golden cup oak" which is applied to this tree. Interior live oak cups are not noticeably hairy, and neither are the undersides of the leaves, young leaves of canyon live oak, however, have a yellow down on their underside.

At all seasons the dense, dark green, dome-shaped form of interior live oak is easy to recognize on the dry western foothills of the Sierra. Typically these trees attain 30-50 feet in height and are composed of many large branches that spread out in all directions, hiding the trunk so that the tree looks like a hemisphere of foliage resting on the ground. *Interior live oak forms orchard-like groves in the foothill grasslands and occupies the chaparral belt mostly between 1500 and 4000 feet. It is also reported growing along Oak Creek on the Sierra desert slope west of Independence.*

In most areas interior live oak hybridizes with black oak to produce a small evergreen tree that has long leaves (2-5 inches) with shallow but pointed lobes. The descriptive common name "evergreen black oak" has been applied to this hybrid, known technically as *Quercus* x *moreha*, but "oracle oak" is now the accepted common name. Its derivation relates to the Latin name which is based upon the Scriptural "land of Moriah" — dwelling place of Abram, founder of Judaism.

The small, dark green trees seen clinging to sheer granite walls of Hetch-Hetchy, Yosemite, Kings, and Kern Canyons are canyon live oaks. In boulder piles beneath the cliffs, in gorges, and near the plunging waterfalls, canyon live oak forms nearly pure groves of spreading trees. John Muir called this species "a sturdy mountaineer of a tree" and he added that, "In tough, unwedgeable, knotty strength, it is the oak of oaks, a magnificent tree."

California settlers praised the quality of its wood, calling it "maul oak" and "hickory oak." The wood, most valuable of any from the western oaks, is heavy (54 lb./cubic ft. air dry), hard, strong, and stiff. It was used for mauls; wagon axles, tongues, and wheels; tool handles; ship's knees; furniture and floors; and wedges for splitting redwood logs into railroad ties. As one might well suspect, canyon live oak wood is close grained, and the trees are slow-growing and long lived.

Although trees among the cliffs and rockpiles seldom burn, tree and shrubby forms of this species also grow on exposed ridges and chaparral slopes that are frequently swept by lightning fires, and, like many of the chaparral shrubs, canyon live oak stumps resprout after burning. Canyon live oak ranges from the rugged terrain of southwestern Oregon through California to mountains of Arizona and northern Mexico. *It grows in abundance along the west slope of the southern Sierra, and occupies the southern canyons [south from Bairs Creek] on the desert slope.*

In favorable sites it attains 50-80 feet in height and three or more feet in diameter. An exceptional tree, known as the Jordan Oak, more than 10 feet thick and with a maximum crown spread of 109 feet grows in the Stanislaus National Forest nine miles southeast of Groveland. Still larger was the canyon live oak growing at the foot of Duckwall Mountain, Tuolumne County, which, after perhaps 600-700 years of existence, was finally toppled by a snow storm in 1965.

Foliage of canyon live oak provides a home for more than 50 species of gall-forming insects, which in turn serve as food for many of the Sierra's 150 species of birds. The acorn crop helps support a variety of animals including band-tailed pigeons who can swallow the acorns whole and let their powerful gizzards do the shelling. As the trees get old and partially rotten, cavities in the trunk provide homes for many creatures. Fungi, ants, and grubs found in dying trees provide still more food for dwellers of the Sierra woodlands.

73

California sycamore

Platanus racemosa
Sycamore family (*Platanaceae*)

Sycamore is one of the most distinctive and interesting trees in the Sierra foothills. Even new visitors to the streams and canyons can recognize California sycamore easily by any of a number of its unusual characteristics. It forms a medium-sized tree largely confined to stream beds and washes. Its spreading but open crown is made up of branches that grow in a crooked or zig-zag manner.

Above the first few feet, the bole and large spreading limbs are covered with smooth bark that continually flakes off, giving it a mottled pattern of whitish, gray, brownish, and pale-green. This shredding results from the bark's inability to expand as the trunk grows, and appears to be a primitive characteristic among broad-leaved trees. Bark in the upper crown is chalky white, and during the short foothill winter, when foliage is off, this makes the tree stand out even when viewed from far away. Sycamores or plane-trees grow in many parts of the Northern Hemisphere and fossils indicate that their progenitors were widely distributed in Arctic regions during the Cretaceous and Tertiary epochs at least 100 million years ago.

Much more recently, in ancient Greece, sycamore was widely planted as the preferred shade tree. The generous shadow cast by the California sycamore's foliage is used by wildlife, livestock, and humans caught out in summer's searing heat. The leaves are light yellow-green and, like maple, are palmately lobed. Sycamore leaves are much thicker than maple leaves and are arranged alternately along the twigs — maples have opposite leaves. California sycamore leaves are from 5 to 11 inches long and about equally wide, and they have three to five long, pointed lobes.

Because of its decorative flowers and fruits this tree has been called "buttonball" or "buttonwood." Each inflorescence consists of about four or five spherical clusters of male or female flowers hanging on a cord-like twig. Female flowers develop into bristly fruit heads nearly an inch in diameter. Both flowers and fruits look like a string of balls.

On the west slope of the Sierra, California sycamore is generally confined to streamsides and washes below about 3000 feet. It also inhabits the Coast Range, but does not grow along the Sierra desert slope or in deserts of southeastern California. However, a similar species known as Arizona sycamore (Platanus wrightii) prospers in arroyos on some of driest mountains in the Sonoran Desert. American sycamore (Platanus occidentalis), the third and best-known plane-tree on this continent, grows in fertile bottomland sites from the Atlantic Coast to the Mississippi Valley.

California sycamores can be seen along the Middle Fork of the Kaweah River near the main entrance to Sequoia National Park; they are abundant in the lower Kaweah drainage south and east of Visalia. Another good place to find them is along the churning Kings River and its tributaries above Pine

California sycamore
Platanus racemosa

Flat Reservoir in Sierra National Forest. These marble-barked, twisted trees often attain heights of 40-60 feet and diameters of two or three feet; but occasionally they grow much larger. The biggest one known grows near Santa Barbara and is reported to be 8½ feet thick, 116 feet tall, and 158 feet in maximum crown spread (as of 1945). This great tree presumably could shade half a football field!

California-laurel

Umbellularia californica
Laurel family (*Lauraceae*)

California-laurel, Oregon-myrtle, California-bay, and pepperwood are names commonly applied to *Umbellularia californica*, the only member of the laurel family (*Lauraceae*) native to the American West. Both the laurel and myrtle families are made up of trees whose foliage and bark contains pungently aromatic oils, and California-laurel is certainly no exception. The "bay leaves" sold in the West as a kitchen spice come from this tree rather than the bay-laurel of Europe, originally used for this purpose. The evergreen leaves of California-laurel give off a strong, camphor-like odor when crushed or bruised.

This is one tree not to seek shelter beneath during a storm. As early as 1826 the botanist-explorer David Douglas discovered that the wind-thrashed foliage gives off an odor so strong it can cause violent sneezing. It is not surprising that California-laurel belongs to the same family as the Oriental "camphor" and tropical "cinnamon" tree, and that its principal North American relative is the spicy sassafras tree of the eastern United States.

California-laurel grows in shady, cool sites along the coast of southern Oregon and California and extends into the mountains via draws and canyons. It thus inhabits the western slope of the southern Sierra to 5000 feet. Here this handsome evergreen forms a giant shrub or small, spreading tree. It can be distinguished from the evergreen oaks by its smooth-margined, fragrant leaves and its green, olive-like fruit.

Various California Indians made use of these "peppernuts" by shelling and eating them or grinding them into meal for making small cakes. In either case the bitterness had to be neutralized by roasting them. Bay leaf tea was used by trappers and Indians as a treatment for stomach and headaches, and to remedy chill. The volatile leaf oils induce perspiration and were employed by Indians and white settlers in steam baths as well as in rubbing compounds for rheumatism. Among other uses, the California Indians also employed the leaves as a household repellent for fleas. Sierra Indian braves made hunting bows from this tree. California-laurel fruit is also eaten by rodents and hogs, giving the latter a peculiar flavor as a result.

Unlike seeds of most Sierra trees, those of California-laurel need not lie dormant over the winter, but often germinate in October, soon after falling. Some of the fruits drop into swollen streams and are swept along, eventually to be cast up on a stony bank or gravel bar where they germinate. The tree also reproduces through sprouts from the root collar, and old fallen trees sprout anew from the stump.

Although it seldom grows to 40 feet in height in the Merced, Kings, Kaweah, or other Sierra drainages, California-laurel forms a huge broadleaf tree with a dense, dome-shaped crown in sheltered sites along the coast of northern California and southern Oregon. Its beautiful tan wood, especially wavy-grained sections cut from burls, are extensively marketed as

California-laurel
Umbellularia californica

bowls, lampbases, etc. of "Oregon myrtle." The scarcity of great spreading "myrtle" trees, however, should demand that they be cut only sparingly, with the realization that the living trees are more magnificent and certainly more necessary to man and the community of living things than novelties produced from them.

bigleaf maple

Acer macrophyllum
Maple family (*Aceraceae*)

Although several species of maple trees are prominent members of the Eastern hardwood forests, only one large maple grows naturally in western North America. Bigleaf maple inhabits the Pacific Coast lowlands and moist, lower mountainsides from the southern tip of the Alaska Panhandle, where it is apparently limited by cold, to southern California, where lack of moisture seems to be the critical factor. It has the largest leaves (6 to 12 inches across) of any American maple, and is robust in other ways also. In the Pacific Northwest its 3 to 4 foot thick trunk often supports a massive, spreading crown, sometimes laden with drapes of hanging clubmoss.

On the west slope of southern Sierra, bigleaf maple is near its southern range limit. Here an equally appropriate name for it would be "canyon maple" since it is largely restricted to moist, shady sites in the depths of the Sierran gorges. It is a common inhabitant of streamsides and cool, canyon rockpiles between 2000 and 5000 feet elevation.

In addition to the large, palmately-lobed maple-like leaves, bigleaf maple can be identified by its opposite leaf arrangement and hence opposite leaf-scars on the stout twigs in winter. The fruit, like that of other maples, is known as a double samara and consists of two nuts with long wings attached in a horseshoe-shaped fashion. These are produced in prolific quantities and some of them hang on the trees all winter, providing nutritious food for various seed-eating birds when pickings are generally scarce.

Springtime visitors to Sierra canyons can see bigleaf maple in its most colorful season. In late April and early May the translucent new leaves are only half-grown while copious clusters of fragrant yellow blossoms 4 to 6 inches long hang from the sunlit boughs. A variety of insects can be observed on warm spring days gathering nectar, and pollinating the maple blossoms in the process.

At the same time of year, countless maple seeds from last season's crop can be found germinating underfoot. In cities, maple seeds germinate profusely in cracks in the streets and sidewalks. In the forest perhaps only one in a million of the new seedlings will encounter favorable conditions — roots must reach moist mineral soil — and live to produce a large tree. Bigleaf maples may survive as long as 200 years, especially in the moist, mild climate along the north Pacific Coast. According to the U. S. Department of Agriculture, bigleaf maple produces maple sugar in nearly as good quality and quantity as eastern sugar maple.

Mountain maple, *Acer glabrum*, (sometimes called Sierra or dwarf maple) grows as a multi-stemmed shrub 10-15 feet tall on rather moist mountainsides usually between 5000 and 9000 feet elevation on both slopes of the southern Sierra. It can be distinguished by its tiny (1-2½ inches wide) maple leaves and often bright-reddish bud and twigs, the latter having opposite leaf scars. Clumps of mountain maple appear to be pruned, which in fact they are. Their twigs are a favorite food of mule deer. The small leaves may be fringed with bright red during growing season because of a blight or fungus.

bigleaf maple
Acer macrophyllum

California buckeye

Aesculus californica
Buckeye family
(*Hippocastanaceae*)

"What was that little round tree at the foot of the mountains covered with clusters of white blossoms about the size and shape of a banana?" This is a question familiar to any ranger or receptionist who has manned an entrance station or information desk in the national parks or forests of the southern Sierra. California buckeye is the bushy foothill tree so beautifully clothed in creamy (or pale rose) flowers that even a casual observer is likely to ask about it.

The fact that it is still blooming so gloriously on the hot foothill slopes late in June (or even into July) when other flowers are wilting further sets buckeye apart. Also, in contrast to other trees and shrubs, it sheds its foliage in midsummer. Apparently this buckeye, whose relatives grow in moister climates, has adapted to the long, dry foothill summers by entering dormancy early. When the leaves have fallen, pear-shaped fruits become obvious dangling from the gaunt branches. The fruit prompted early settlers to call this squatty little tree "California pear."

That this appellation was made tongue in cheek will be apparent to anyone who stops to investigate the tree and its fruit. The "pear" is actually a leathery husk that envelopes a shiny brown seed 1-2 inches across. The glossy seed showing from the yellowish husk is reminiscent of the eye of a deer, hence the name "buckeye." It may seem strange that a tree bearing clusters of flowers produces solitary fruits; however only one flower from each group matures and produces a seed.

Several other species of buckeyes

(or horsechestnuts) are native to the eastern United States including Ohio, the "Buckeye State." The seed of California buckeye resembles that of the commonly cultivated European horsechestnut tree (*Aesculus hippocastanum*). So do the leaves, which are made up of 5-7 palmately arranged leaflets. Leaves of California buckeye emerge so early in spring that they are sometimes blanketed with a heavy wet snowfall that weights down and breaks the boughs. As with horsechestnut, the leaves are attached in an opposite pattern; the blossoms appear similar except in not usually being pink, and the raw seeds are also poisonous to man or beast. Seeds of buckeye are rarely eaten by wildlife, a situation presumably advantageous to the tree's reproduction. Nectar of California buckeye flowers is known to poison bees!

Resourceful California Indians capitalized on the buckeye's lethal properties by using it to catch fish. They ground up seeds and poured them into a pool in the stream, then picked up the stupefied fish which floated to the surface. Perhaps more

seed pod

Surprising is the fact that Sierra Indians used buckeye seeds for food. They ground the nuts and leached them repeatedly with water until at last the toxicity was dispelled; then they cooked and ate the nutritious meal.

California buckeye grows only in its namesake State, from Siskiyou and Shasta Counties to northern Los Angeles and Kern Counties. *It occupies the western slopes of the southern Sierra mostly between 1000 and 3000 feet elevation where it is found in abundance as a large ball-shaped shrub or small tree 10-25 feet tall growing among chaparral shrubs, canyon live oaks, and Digger pines.*

California buckeye
Aesculus californica

ash

Fraxinus spp.
Olive family (*Oleaceae*)

Although three species of ash inhabit canyons and ravines on the lower slopes of the southern Sierra, few people are familiar with even one of them. Not that the ashes are hard to distinguish from other trees. They can be identified by large, oppositely arranged leaves composed of 3 to 7 oval leaflets, as well as by their hanging clusters of inch-long winged fruits. Ashes bear "samaras" like those of maple except that the latter are fused together in pairs to make a V-shaped double samara. Ashes have single samaras.

The reason Sierra ashes are so little-known seems partly attributable to their scarcity and partly to their small, inconspicuous, form. One of these species, Oregon ash (*Fraxinus latifolia*), attains heights up to 100 feet or more in Oregon's moist Willamette Valley; however in our region of the Sierra it is approaching its southern range limits. Here, this northwestern hardwood is largely confined to streamside in the canyons below 5000 feet, and even then produces only scattered, crooked trees less than 25 feet tall. *Oregon ash is reported to occupy most of the western slope of the Sierra; locally it is noted growing along the Merced River near El Portal.*

About 16 species of ash grow in North America, mostly in the East, and all but one are trees. *Flowering ash (Fraxinus dipetala), which grows only in California is the exception. It forms an arborescent shrub with numerous, slender stems usually 5-15 feet high, growing on the western slope of the southern Sierra between about 1500 and 3500 feet. In addition to having a low growth-form this ash is distinguished by its showy blossoms that appear with the leaves in spring.*

The technical name meaning "two-petaled ash" describes the individual flowers, which are borne in clusters. This little ash can be found locally in the Sequoia-Kings Canyon vicinity at Ash Mountain, Elk Creek, west of Panorama Point, and in lower Kings Canyon.

Leatherleaf or desert ash (*Fraxinus velutina* var. *coriacea*) is a native of the Southwest's desert canyons. Its range extends westward from Arizona into the arid regions of southern California. *It grows along streams in the southernmost portion of the Sierra's desert slope, west of Owens Lake, up to 5600 feet elevation.* Leatherleaf ash's Sierra habitat lies only 50 miles west of the harshest of all North American deserts. This species also ekes out an existence in canyons of the Panamint Range bordering Death Valley itself. It grows slowly, attaining a height of 20-30 feet in a form suggestive more of its distant relative the ancient Mediterranean olive tree than the straight, tall ash of the eastern United States.

Fraxinus dipetala

Pacific dogwood

Cornus nuttallii
Dogwood family
(*Cornaceae*)

Pacific dogwood is the most beautiful flowering tree gracing the West Coast's conifer forests. In May or early June it stands out beneath the giant Douglas-firs, sugar pines, or sequoias because its leafless branches are laden with creamy white blossoms several inches across. By September the flowers have developed into clusters of bright red berry-like fruits nestled among green, orange, or scarlet leaves, and sometimes a second crop of white blossoms has appeared.

This showy little tree is especially unusual because it typically grows in the somber shade at the foot of giant conifers, a habitat in which few other hardwoods can survive. Studies of the closely related eastern dogwood have revealed part of this species' secret of success in growing beneath such a dense forest canopy: dogwood carries out maximum photosynthesis under conditions of only ⅓ of full sunlight.

Pacific dogwood is also known as western flowering dogwood in recognition of its likeness to flowering dogwood (*Cornus florida*), the species indigenous to the eastern United States. The resemblance is so close that David Douglas, the first botanist to see Pacific dogwood, thought it was the eastern species. In the 1830's, a decade after Doug-

Pacific dogwood
Cornus nuttallii

las's visit, the American naturalist Thomas Nuttall examined the beautiful dogwoods of the Pacific Slope and found among other differences that this species has 4-6 petal-like bracts (vs. 4 in eastern dogwood), and that its blossoms measure up to 6 inches in diameter (larger than in the eastern species). Nuttall wrote that although the red berries are somewhat bitter, they are the favorite autumn food of band-tailed pigeons.

Pacific dogwood occupies the moist conifer forests from the southern coast of British Columbia to San Diego County. It forms a slender-trunked, but spreading tree 20-40 feet tall. *Dogwood is well represented in the pine and sequoia forests between about 3500 and 6000 feet elevation on the west slope of the southern Sierra.* It can be distinguished from other hardwoods by its oppositely arranged leaves and twigs; by leaves 3-5 inches long and oval in shape, and by smooth, ashy-gray bark.

Dogwood flowers are actually quite small and inconspicuous. They grow in the head-like cluster or "button" that produces the red fruits. Large white petal-like structures extending from the flower cluster are known as "bracts", and the dogwood blooms are properly called blossoms.

One writer suggests that the name "dogwood" may have been used either in contempt for "worthless timber" or in reference to its astringent bark as a cure for the mange in dogs. Indians of the Pacific Northwest boiled the bark to make a laxative. Also, the tannin-rich bark has been used successfully in place of quinine to cure malaria.

Two very similar species of tall, red-stemmed dogwood shrubs inhabit streamsides between about 4000 and 8000 feet on both slopes of the southern Sierra. One of these is red-osier dogwood (*Cornus stolonifera*), which grows all across the continent; the other is western dogwood (*Cornus occidentalis*). Both are appropriately known as "creek dogwood" in the Sierra, where they occur together and sometimes hybridize. Creek dogwoods also have 2-4 inch long oval leaves and twigs arranged oppositely. Equally distinctive features are their bright red bark and beautiful clusters of small white flowers. These make a pleasant color contrast with the bright green foliage and the sparkling mountain stream so often found gushing over their roots. Still another shrubby dogwood, *Cornus glabrata*, is reported to occupy moist sites below 5000 feet on the west slope of the southern Sierra.

wild cherry
Prunus spp.

mountain-mahogany
Cercocarpus spp.
Rose family (*Rosaceae*)

Three species of wild cherry and two of mountain-mahogany sometimes grow as arborescent shrubs in the southern Sierra. All of these species are members of the Rose family (*Rosaceae*), which includes such familiar trees as the cherry, apricot, and peach (all *Prunus* spp.) as well as apple, pear, hawthorne, and mountain-ash.

Bitter cherry (*Prunus emarginata*) often develops in large thickets 10 or 15 feet tall bordering rockpiles, meadows, or other openings in the cool Jeffrey pine and red fir forest. *Its thickets are most commonly found between about 4500 and 9000 feet on both slopes of the southern Sierra.* In July these little groves are covered with a profusion of white flowers, and are characterized by the steady buzzing of bees and other pollinating insects. The flowers impart an almond-like fragrance to the surrounding air, and by autumn have developed into clusters of shiny, bright red cherries that look quite appetizing.

However, the fruits are so intensely bitter that squirrels, bears, and many birds are reported to eat them only sparingly. Bitter cherry can be further distinguished by its grayish bark that gives off a distinct cherry odor when bruised, by new twigs that

bitter cherry
Prunus emarginata

are reddish, and by alternately arranged oval leaves that have one or two small but conspicuous glands at the base of the blade.

Western chokecherry (*Prunus virginiana* var. *demissa*) develops as a tall shrub (occasionally to 20 feet) mostly between about 2000 and 6000 feet elevation on the western slope of the southern Sierra. Chokecherry's white flowers are borne in compact, cylindrical clusters 3-5 inches long that often attract the attention of visitors to the Sierra. The flowers mature into small grape-like clusters of purplish cherries which are edible, but have an astringent aftertaste alluded to in the name "chokecherry".

The leaves, like those of bitter cherry, have one or two small glands, but these are usually situated on the petiole rather than on the blade. Also, chokecherry leaves have pointed tips, while those of bitter cherry are rounded. Chokecherry foliage is a favorite food of deer and elk throughout much of the West, and the ripe cherries are eagerly devoured by many species of birds. Indians used the fruits fresh or dried, in the latter case pounding them into a meal which was mixed with dried meat to make pemmican. Chokecherries are

gathered by modern Californians for jellies and jams, and occasionally for wine.

When growing in stony or sandy soil, Klamath or Sierra plum (*Prunus subcordata*) generally forms a shrub less than 10 feet tall; however in valley bottoms or other favorable sites it grows as a small tree 15-20 feet tall and half a foot thick. *This wild plum usually grows in the vicinity of streams and is found between about 4000 and 6000 feet on the western slope of the southern Sierra. It is distinguished from bitter cherry and chokecherry by its thorn-like twigs as well as by its edible although somewhat tart plum ¾ to 1 inch long. It is scarcer than the wild cherries but can be seen in several locations including the highway near Wawona, at Big Meadow, and at Hetch Hetchy in Yosemite National Park, as well as in Kings Canyon, Grant Grove, and Whitaker Forest.*

Two species of mountain-mahogany inhabit the Sierra. Birchleaf mountain-mahogany (*Cercocarpus betuloides*) usually forms a shrub under 10 feet in height and grows on the driest, rocky slopes and washes in the foothills of the Sierra west slope. Curl-leaf mountain mahogany (*Cercocarpus ledifolius*).

bitter cherry
Prunus emarginata

ordinarily grows as a small, crooked, single-stemmed tree 12-20 feet high and 6-8 inches in diameter. Widely distributed in the arid West, in the Sierra it inhabits only the desert, east slope. Here it can be found growing on exposed, south-facing slopes and hot, dry, rocky ridges from 5000 to slightly higher than 10,000 feet.

Its common names describe this little desert tree quite well. "Desert mountain-mahogany" refers to its mountainous, arid habitat and to the reddish brown wood. "Ironwood" applies to the close-grained, very dense wood, which is exceedingly hard and heavy. "Curl-leaf" describes the way the evergreen leaves are rolled under at their margins; the leaves average about an inch long and ¼ inch wide. "Plume-tree" relates to the long, silky plume-like fruits that cover the crown of these craggy little trees during late-summer and fall.

mountain mahogany
Cercocarpus ledifolius

Eastward from the Sierra in the dry ranges of the Great Basin, curl-leaf mountain-mahogany sometimes forms a woodland zone on the mountainsides between the belt of pinyons and junipers below, and the limber and bristlecone pines on the summits. Wherever mountain-mahogany is found from the canyons of central Idaho to the Sierra east escarpment to high mountains of Baja California, it provides shade, shelter, and choice year-round forage for mule deer, and often for bighorn sheep as well.

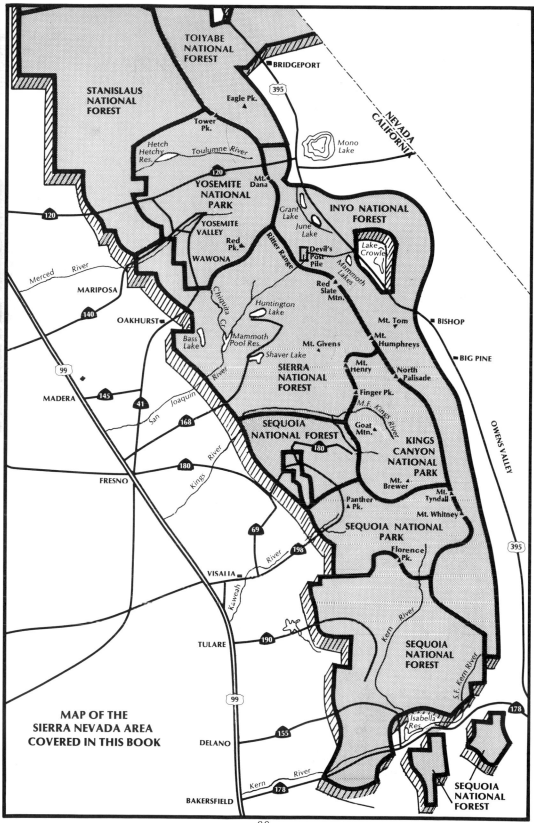

MAP OF THE
SIERRA NEVADA AREA
COVERED IN THIS BOOK

Author

Stephen F. Arno came to know the Sierra trees in the mid 1960's when he spent two summers as a naturalist at Sequoia and Kings Canyon National Parks. In the years that followed he completed detailed research projects on trees of the timberline and earned a Ph.D. in 1970. He is currently employed as a forest ecologist by the U. S. Forest Service.

Artist

Cover and text illustrations for Discovering Sierra Trees are by Jane Gyer, an artist in the Yosemite area since 1956. Her lifelong fascination with tree forms and designs has influenced much of her creative work.